The Apocalypse then GLORY!

By
Ken Wooldridge

Copyright © 2012 by Ken Wooldridge.
All rights reserved.

This book may not be reproduced in any form without the written permission of the publisher Ken Wooldridge. All Scripture quotations are from – The original King James version of the Bible.

Publisher:
Ken Wooldridge
P.O. Box 7312,
Knoxville, TN 37921, USA
www.kenwooldridge.org

First printing in 2012

ISBN-10: 0979022037
EAN-13: 9780979022036

Library of Congress Control Number: 2012934343
Kenneth Wooldridge, Knoxville, TN
Printed by CreateSpace, North Charleston, SC in the USA

Cover design – Michael Dutton

Book dedication:

*I dedicate this book
to my lovely wife Marie
with whom I have spent
a lifetime of precious memories!*

The purpose of this book

In 1977 I had a death experience.
Other revelations and visions followed.
I was also blessed to hear the testimonies of others.
It has caused me to spend much time in
contemplation and prayer about the subject.
Finally I feel it is the right time to present this book
for your reading pleasure.
I have written it in the form of a novel.
I trust that the future prophetical events will
become clear as they unfold before your eyes.

The first part of the book deals with the Apocalypse
and is frightening.
However the second part should bring surprise,
wonder and excitement.
By reading this book, you will be confronted with –
- World events that are about to happen.
- Powerful players in the end time drama.
- Dangers many will face.
- How your life may be affected.
- How you may prepare yourself.
- How you can ensure your salvation and escape.
- Amazing glories that await every true Christian.

If you enjoy reading this book, please tell your loved ones and friends about it.

Contents:

Chapter One
Hell on earth 1

Chapter Two
The Antichrist and his World Government 9

Chapter Three
The False Prophet, Two Witnesses and
horrific times 25

Chapter Four
The magnificent Jewish Temple, Persecution
and Martyrdom 37

Chapter Five
Heaven bound 57

Chapter Six
Heaven 69

Chapter Seven
The Marriage of the Lamb 89

Chapter Eight
The Millennial reign of Jesus Christ and His Bride 95

Chapter Nine
The New Jerusalem. 103

Chapter Ten
The City of Jerusalem on Earth. 119

Chapter Eleven
The Wedding Feast 135

Chapter Twelve
Life in the New Jerusalem 157

Chapter Thirteen
Entering Eden 165

Conclusion

Part One

Part One

Chapter One

Hell On Earth

It was horrific to watch the News last night and I did so with trepidation.
The world was spiraling in what seemed to be a never ending path of destruction.
It seems to be the beginning of Hell on earth.
We knew that the Bible predicted this and also a glorious future that would follow!

Catastrophic birth pains seemed to pulsate up and down on the East and West of the globe.
These catastrophes took the form of Earthquakes, Hurricanes and Tsunamis.

It all started with a world economic meltdown and a worldwide economic depression.
Then the fatal financial crash came.
Most banks failed, and large or small corporations were bankrupted.
Millions of helpless people lost their jobs and had no financial income.

THE APOCALYPSE THEN GLORY

They had no money to pay their rent, utilities or buy food.
They waited in vain for the Government to come to their rescue.

The crises was so great and the food kitchens so few and far between.
Most people became poverty stricken overnight and many families went to bed hungry at night.
It then became chaotic in the streets.
There was rioting and looting of stores.

It was terrible to watch the rising smoke of burning buildings and shopping centers.
It was too widespread that the Police, National Guard and Military had no control.
Robberies, violence and murders were rampant everywhere.
People were desperate to get food, supplies and gasoline.
Many pacifying speeches were made by the national and local government officials.
These seemed empty and ineffective.
We knew that it would take a long time to organize food provisions and assistance to the needy.
We came together in our neighborhood and organized help and protection for ourselves.
All roads into our area were guarded and our streets were watched by the neighborhood.

Then a unified Government of all the Political Parties was formed.
It declared a national State of Emergency.
Many internet and phone communication systems had failed.

The remaining internet, television, radio and phone companies were nationalized by Congress.
It was what seemed to be an unending six months of chaos.
Then an announcement was made that the world leaders had completed a World Summit Meeting.
They formed a New World Government in an effort to rescue the world from chaos.
A President was elected as the World Leader.
He was from France and his name was Benoit Chevalier.
This was quickly and overwhelmingly ratified by the Governments of every nation.
This was welcomed by most people who assumed that it was the Worlds only possible solution.
The national borders of the different countries vanished overnight.
All the people of the world were given equal world citizenship.
Shortly thereafter, the World Government Leader made a televised appearance.
He announced that a new World financial System had been formulated.
It took three months of intensive work by millions of Programmers and IT Technicians to implement it.
A super computer in Belgium was linked to computer centers in every major city of the world.
From there links were created to every City, Town and Home.

Every person was given a cash card with a special drawing right.
It enabled them to have a certain amount of money on their card every month.

I also received such a card, and so did everyone I knew.
The first day of each month, the equivalent of $2000.00 was pended to my card.
The card was similar to a credit card.
Whatever I bought, or service I paid for was subtracted off that card during the month.
When I bought groceries or other items at the Store I paid with my card.
Similarly paying for the utilities, phone or gas at the gas station was the same way.
Obviously it was very convenient and immediately removed all anxiety and poverty.
Most people welcomed it and were excited about it.
However, it didn't take long for fraudulent activity to follow.
There was the theft and duplication of cards and people everywhere began to suffer loss.
There was an outcry for the system to be changed.
Then a TV announcement came one evening.
The Word Government was responding to the outcry of the people.
They were implementing a significant change.

Every citizen would receive a computer chip implant that would take the place of the cash card. It would be inserted under the skin in one of two places on the body.

The insertion would be either on the top of the right hand or on the forehead.
It would allow easy access and be convenient for electronic scanning.
This microchip would contain all the private and medical information of each individual.

It would be scanned whenever a purchase was made, visiting a hospital or clinic.
The inserted chip was the solution that would eliminate fraud.
Most people were jubilant, immediately finding their way to a Center to receive it.
They lined up and waited diligently to receive their implants.

I found myself amongst a small group of people, who recognized this as the Mark of the Beast.

It was predicted in the Bible –

"He causes all, both small and great, rich and poor, free and bond, to receive a mark in their right hand, or in their foreheads: And that no man might buy or sell, save he that had the mark, or the name of the beast, or the number of his name. Here is wisdom. Let him that hath understanding count the number of the beast: for it is the number of a man; and his number is Six hundred threescore and six."
Revelation 13:16-18

All of us immediately began to stock up on as much food and supplies as we could.
We were small home groups of Christians made up of family and friends.
Each of the families noted what groceries and other supplies they had.
Then we carefully assessed what our anticipated needs would be.
This included food, personal needs, clothing, vehicles, homes and other things.
We planned and worked on sources of supply.

We contacted farmers and others where we were able to directly buy or barter what we needed.
Most everyone started outdoor or indoor vegetable gardens.
Some started raising chickens and hens.
Several Christian farmers were raising goats and cows for milk and cheese.
Some were breeding cattle and hogs for meat.
During summer we got busy canning the overstock of fruit and vegetables.
We also dehydrated what we had and foraged for later use.
All of this served to be lifesaving later.

Suddenly, without warning, the world received shocking News.
Russia in alliance with Muslim countries had declared war on Israel.
They were quickly advancing with their armies for a devastating attack.
There was an outcry and warning from the World Government.
This was completely disregarded and ignored.
They were close to the borders around Israel and set for the final assault.
It seemed inevitable that Israel would be annihilated.

We all watched hour by hour television reports and images.
The World was in fear of what would follow.
Then the television reports and images suddenly changed and revealed just the opposite.
Israel had ferociously responded and deployed weapons of mass destruction.

It effectively destroyed their enemies within one hour.
They used tactical nuclear and laser weapons.
Their enemies were wiped out in a mushroom cloud bloodbath.

Immediately the world was thrust into Political chaos and there were outcries from everywhere.
The Muslim world and Eastern Europe were in disarray.
This event was sure to have devastating and far reaching global and ecological affects.

Chapter Two

The Antichrist and his World Government

A person began to receive great respect and notoriety, in world politics.
His appearance had come at a time of world chaos.
His name was Muhammad Reza Shahanshah.
I was told that his name meant three things namely –
A descendant of Muhammad
King of Kings
One who is loved.

The Muslims had received a humiliating defeat by Israel.
They were war devastated, in derision, confusion and poverty.

With perfect timing and great wisdom Muhammad Reza Shahanshah reached out to help them.
They were quickly regrouped under his leadership.
After a while they all began to refer to him as their Mhadi.
He was a charismatic leader with a genial mind.
Within a year, his leadership restored to them a sense of pride.
He reminded them that they were a part of the great Persian Empire.
He exercised great subtlety and prowess in everything he did.

In a relatively short period he achieved great Political and Economical success.
His achievements gained him great respect, favor and the support of World Leaders.
He was asked to be a part of their great Alliance.
This enabled him to make suggestions and intellectual contributions.

Soon thereafter he was appointed as a Member of the World Government.
The plans he presented were dynamic and executed with great success.
Within months he was proclaimed as the one who would solve the world problems.
He was certain to rescue it from chaos and there was no other leader like him.
There also seemed to be an uncanny force helping him to success.
We knew that it was satan.

Within our Christian community, there was no doubt that we were seeing the rise of the Antichrist.

Soon thereafter he was elected as the World Government President.
A spectacular ceremony was held, viewed around the world.
He was inducted into his position.

His first act of Office was to sign a seven year contract with all the nations of the world.
It was a lengthy contract offering peace, protection and prosperity to them.
In return they committed their loyalty to him and support of his plans.
This included an agreement with Israel, which he later broke after 3½ years.
This occurred when he went to sit in their Holy of Holies as God, and they rejected him.

Things all around the world quickly began to change.
It was almost impossible to report and keep up with all the changes.
New laws and customs were being promulgated and instituted daily.
This happened on the International Front,
throughout every Country and in every Community.

The following Holidays were removed -
Christmas,
Easter,
Memorial Day,
Independence Day,
Labor Day,
Thanksgiving.

New holidays were instituted:
World Presidents Day – celebrating the Antichrist.
Day of light – celebrating the God of this World (We knew that referred to Lucifer)
New World Day – celebrating the founding of the New World Government.
Equality Day – celebrating the equality and oneness of Mankind.
Gaia Day – celebrating the mother earth Goddess.
On each of these new holidays, the world celebrated and gave gifts to each other.

The world became so strange, different and uncomfortable.
I honestly felt that I was living on another planet.
We often reminisced and spoke of the good old days, when life was so open and free.
We savored the time when we lived in abundance.
Now suspicion and mistrust ruled the day and caused much confusion and hurt.

Many other areas were affected by laws that were passed.
Local Churches were compelled to be licensed with the authorities.
They were enforced to furnish the State Government a membership list each year.
They wanted to know who attended what church.
The tax exemption status benefiting churches was removed.
Churches were forced to pay property tax.
They lost their subsidy programs and that increased their financial obligations.
Contributors could no longer get tax deductions for their financial contributions to Churches.

The financial income decreased and many churches were devastated.

A new law was passed that effected Pastors.
They could only be Ordained and State licensed if they had a Masters Degree education.
In addition they had to complete a continued education class on Ministry requirements each year. It was presented by a World Church Representative. Inevitably many Pastors became government pleasers and informants.

Then it became illegal to preach the Gospel in public places or evangelize from door to door. Proselyting people from one religion to another was strictly forbidden.
Sharing the Gospel with children became a federal crime.
It was punishable with a minimum five year jail sentence.

Christian television and radio programs went off the air due to a lack of financial support. Stringent laws restricted the contents of their programs.

Marriage licensing by sexual orientation was replaced by marriage partnership agreements.
Being married to more than one person at a time, no longer was regarded as unlawful polygamy.
Long term marriage commitments disappeared and were renewable every five years.
Bisexual and Heterosexual couples lived together and with the slightest disagreement, moved on to other partners.

Because of a diminishing life expectancy, a shortage of men began to occur and several women began to share one male partner.

In Family situations, Father and Mother roles became insignificant.
The State automatically assumed the Legal Guardianship of children, second to the parents.
Each community took the responsibility of overseeing the raising of the community children.
The Parents were held answerable to them.
Later in the tribulation many parents died as a result of the rampant viruses and diseases.
Children became orphaned and destitute and they lived from home to home.

Obesity outside of medical causes was declared an offence.
Those found guilty had to attend counseling.
It was defined by height and weight stipulations and many became victims of discrimination.
Fines were imposed upon parents whose children were negligently obese.
New scientifically formulated, enriched foods began to replace everyday basic foods.
Because of food shortages, televised programs indoctrinated people to follow the new food diets.
In many places people were encouraged to eat only two meals a day.
A brunch at 11 am and a dinner at 5 pm.

A crashing world economy caused failing companies to be nationalized by the Government.
Only one kind of Company was allowed for each specific product or service.

This applied to computers, software, hardware, utilities, phones, internet, vehicles, building supplies and manufacturing.
Competition was eliminated and many well known brand names disappeared.

Private ownership of Property, Homes, Buildings and Corporations were eliminated.
Everyone worked for the Government.

In the work force, much emphasis was placed on cleaning and restoring the environment.
Many new environmental jobs became available.
The government committed a seven year period and great financial resources to achieve this.

Teams of workers were sent out to repair houses and buildings.
They first concentrated working in earthquake, flood and hurricane affected areas.
Workers were also used to clean up oil spills, chemical contamination and pollution.

Farming and producing food became huge and highly specialized.
New solar, wind and other energy industries evolved.
These were also government controlled, and many workers were employed in these new areas.

Due to impending dangers, many people were reluctant to travel on vacation.
This negatively affected the business of major airline carriers and Hotel resorts.

Many closed and others were dramatically downsized.
Laws were passed that made it more difficult to travel internationally.
Restrictions were imposed on the duration of travel.
Stringent passenger health and weight requirements disqualified many.

Often we talked about the wonderful places we had visited.
We remembered the departures and arrivals at the airports.
The times we travelled to visit with our loved ones.
The wonderful vacations we had at the beach, the luxury and enjoyment of the vacation resorts. This was all something of the past.

Many of our children and grandchildren experienced other kinds of disappointments.
Their dreams of going to College and graduating with a College Degree were curtailed.
Many distinguished Universities and Colleges closed down because of financial difficulties.
This made it almost impossible to find a College and get accepted on campus.
Young people were encouraged to join the world workforce and do part time online studies.
Only those who embraced evolution, humanism and atheism were favored for acceptance.

Medical treatment was freely available including those who wanted an abortion.
However the treatment of senior citizens and terminally ill patients became very limited.

The practice of euthanasia was encouraged and strict laws were enacted to facilitate it.
Parents were penalized if they had more than two children.

The Justice system radically changed.
Its purpose was the advancement of the State and Government agenda.
It no longer followed the will of the people.
People were forced to comply or suffer the consequences.
Any sign of dissension or aggression, was met with immediate police or military response.
People resigned themselves to subservience, suffering weakness and depression.
The courts also became the rubber stamp of the justice system.
Any kind of reliable legal representation became impossible.
The State and Government frowned on the high cost of incarcerating inmates.
Prisoners were transported to large detention facilities of the State.
There they had to work hard, were poorly fed and clothed.
All other privileges and benefits were taken away.

The world became a cold unemotional place.
Many people were hateful, criminal, dangerous and ruthless.

We knew that time was short.
We could not procrastinate and relentlessly proclaimed our message to the world.

We did it very boldly, sometimes privately and very secretively.
- We preached of the very soon coming of Jesus Christ.
- We warned people not to receive the chip implant, mark of the beast.
- We warned that those who did would suffer greatly and receive eternal damnation.
- We taught the true Doctrine of the Bible.
- We warned people not to listen to and follow false prophets.
- We warned people not to compromise their faith and be a part of the world ecumenical system.
- We invited people to be a part of the Bride of Christ and to be sealed with His Holy Spirit.
- We provided them with Bibles and Spiritual Material.

By doing that, we were forced to break the law.
In spite of that, we felt obligated to follow the commands of God.
We knew that His laws superseded those of man.
We seriously weighed the consequences for our actions and were willing to pay the price.
We prayed and asked God if this was pleasing to Him.
The Holy Spirit gave us this simple answer -
"God would protect us from detection, danger and arrest to do His work.
He created chameleons, insects and flowers that change their color.
They do this to protect themselves from detection and danger.

We would do what we needed to do to accomplish His task and God would protect us."

Many brushed aside what we said and ridiculed us.
Some however, intently gave heed to what we said and attended our home churches.
They were saved, baptized and filled with the Holy Spirit.
They continued building themselves up in the Faith.
There exuberance and joy multiplied.

One of the first major achievements of the Antichrist was his new city called Babylon.
It was considered the greatest city ever built.
It had a spectacular skyline of buildings that could be seen miles away.
They varied in architectural design.
Some were glass mirrored, some of white stone and others of colored marble.
Along the main highway entering the city were hanging gardens like Ancient Babylon.

It boasted having the world's finest hotels and restaurants.
They provided all variations of international cuisine.

Hundreds of ships ported in and out of its harbor each day bringing precious cargo.
Passengers and cargo from all over the world arrived day and night at its magnificent airport.
Merchants came from near and far to buy and sell.
They traded in gold, silver, precious stones, pearls, fabric, silk and precious commodities.
Hundreds of spice vendors displayed and sold all kinds of spice at the World Spice Market.

THE APOCALYPSE THEN GLORY

Customers were attracted to the welcoming oriental fragrances and loved to shop there.

They enjoyed making their selections from the colorful heaps of spices on display.

The Mall of Babylon was the largest of its kind in the world.
It was housed in the world's tallest building.
Its exclusive stores sold perfumes, ointments, oils and vintage wines.
They also specialized in imported products from all over the world.
At the lower level was the world's largest indoor snow skiing resort.

Close by was a large Aquarium with all kinds of sea life on display.
It is celebrated as the planet's largest Aquarium.
It featured 20 major habitats and 50 focus exhibits.
It was home to ocean animals, representing more species than any other.
Its Dolphin shows were amazing.

Nearby was the Gold Market attracting buyers from everywhere.
Large quantities of quality gold, precious stones and jewelry were on display.

Many major sports events were hosted in the Sports Superdome that housed 200.000 people.

The world's most talented musicians and singers came to Babylon.

They were invited to perform in the majestic Tower Symphony and Concert Hall.
It was a round building, symbolic of the Biblical Tower of Babel.

There were art galleries within walking distance all around it.
There famous artists displayed their priceless works of art.
On either side of the four roads that led from it, were shops for craftsmen.
They demonstrated their lathing, sculpting, precious metal casting and engraving skills.

Another popular venue was the New World Museum.
It was ten times the size of the Smithsonian in Washington.
It was admired by the educated and laymen alike.

Then there was the Nature dome, a huge genial architectural masterpiece that covered an area of about ten square miles. In it was replicated the different climates of the world.
It housed many animals, birds, fish and insects of the world.
Its concepts were regarded as experimental, to be used later in outer space travel.

The scientific laboratories of Babylon specialized in every area of science.
Some of the world's leading scientists practiced there.
They conducted great scientific experiments and amazing new discoveries were being made.

The Global Medical Center retained some of the best Specialists and Doctors.
Breathtaking intricate surgeries were being done and medical advances made.
Amazing body transplants were being performed.
These were being telecom-muted throughout the world for educational purposes.
Body parts were being genetically grown and marketed from there for recipients.

Visiting Babylon was a dream for any citizen of the world to experience.
Most people only got to see it in media documentaries or television programs.
Babylon became the seat of the church of the Antichrist.
A huge Temple was built in honor of his False Prophet.
It became the Headquarters of the World Church.
There the Antichrist sat on a golden Throne and was worshipped as God.
This temple was located next to a large lake called Alshefaa Waters.
It had the world's largest dancing water fountain and it shot water up 1000 feet in the air.
At the same time healing music and songs were played in many languages.
In the evening it was dramatically illuminated by pulsating floodlights.
Sick people came there from all over and were administered satanic healing, by Temple Priests.

Nearby there were several large artificial Palm Islands located just off the coast.

They had some of the whitest and sandiest, palm studded beaches.
There was an amazing Marina with coffee shops, restaurants and walkways to visit.
From there yachts came and went, with famous celebrities and travelers throughout the year.
Every time we as Christians saw Babylon on television, we knew that the City was destined for total devastation and that the world would one day mourn its destruction.

Chapter Three

The False Prophet, Two Witnesses and horrific times

During his rise to power, the Antichrist made many enemies among world Illuminati Leaders.
Finally they planned and executed an assassination attempt on his life.
It happened one Friday morning.
He climbed out of his limousine and walked into the World Government Parliament Building.
Suddenly one of his Guards turned toward him and with a concealed short sword, thrust it into his chest. He was rushed to the hospital and was pronounced dead upon arrival.

The World mourned while his enemies celebrated. That night, the False Prophet, as we called him, rushed to the hospital where his corpse lay.

The whole world waited with expectancy to see what would happen.
They knew that he performed great miracles and signs.
The next morning an announcement was made that an important Television appearance was imminent.
The world watched in shock and amazement as the Antichrist was presented alive by the False Prophet.
He announced that he had raised him from the dead in the name of Lucifer.

When the Antichrist spoke, there was something different about him.
His eyes were glowing and he seemed to be satan possessed.

Within weeks, his enemies who perpetrated the crime against him were tracked down.
They were immediately tried and executed by the authorities.
Now the Antichrist was completely in control of world affairs.
Everyone was in awe of him and his authority was unquestioned.
Black magic and sorceries gained popularity and became a part of the Temple ritual.
It was performed by Priests and Temple Virgins dressed in black robes.
It was said that they also participated in human sacrifices and trafficking.
At this time, the Mark of the beast received by most world citizens began to be strictly enforced.
We were all educated by the media of its importance and significance.

It was the only way that one could buy or sell anything.
It also was a pledge of Allegiance to the Antichrist and his Government.
People who refused to receive it were regarded as criminals, rejecting authority.
They were incarcerated and sent away to concentration camps.
There they were only given one chance to recant their Faith and receive the mark.
If they disobeyed they were executed by beheading.

The False Prophet otherwise known as the Holy One, appeared on International Television.
He was introduced by the Chairman of the World Ecumenical Council, Cardinal **Antonio Russo**.
He hailed the Holy One as a man greater than Moses of the Bible.
The False Prophet proclaimed that he had received his ordination from Lucifer.
He would demonstrate his supernatural power to the whole world.
He built a stone altar and placed a live, tied goat on it.
He offered this sacrifice to the Antichrist who he said was god incarnate.
With the stroke of his hand, a lightning bolt of fire came from the sky and consumed the sacrifice.
Then he walked over to a statue that resembled the Antichrist.
He spoke to it and immediately it came to life and spoke eloquently, in praise of the Antichrist.
We knew that he had invoked demon powers to do this.

People revered the False Prophet and hung on every word he spoke.
Each morning a devotional was televised by him and people were called upon to worship the Antichrist.
They gladly did this, because they regarded the Antichrist as the savior and provider of the world.

It became more difficult each day for Christians to endure the hardship.
Life became a matter of survival.
We practiced every aspect of survival we knew and shared information with each other.
People of the world everywhere were suffering from plagues and sicknesses.
However we who were sealed by God were supernaturally protected.
We were invited into the homes of these ailing people and cared for them.
We demonstrated the love of God to them.
In turn many also secretly shared their homes and provisions with us.
In addition God performed wonderful miracles of provision for us.
We always had a place to live, clothing and food to eat.

We always looked forward to the devotional times we had.
We were greatly blessed when we secretly gathered together for worship.
These were wonderful times of singing, Bible reading, prayers, words of exhortation and encouragement. The most longed for occasion was when we enjoyed Holy Communion.

We knew that as the true Bride of Christ, we had been sealed with the Holy Spirit of promise.
Continually the anointing of the Holy Spirit would come upon us.
Our spiritual lamps remained full of oil.
It was a refreshing experience and brought exuberant joy and happiness.
The Holy Spirit kept us faithful, waiting for the soon coming of our Heavenly Bridegroom, Jesus Christ.

Then something happened that greatly encouraged us.
It was the appearance of Moses and Elijah.
They identified themselves as the Two Witnesses of God.
Frequently there were news reports of them appearing all over the world.
Sometimes they spoke to large gatherings and at other times exclusively to small groups in homes.
First they were seen in Israel and then in different countries in Europe.
Then it was reported that they were Ministering in the New York area.
There they mentioned that they were going to Palm Beach and Miami.
We all knew that Gods Two Witnesses had a specific itinerary and agenda.
They would visit a place only once and then travel on.
Their purpose was to visit all the major Jewish communities, throughout the world.

Our Jewish Brother Isaac had been privileged to attend one of these gatherings.

He said that throughout the meeting, he was overwhelmed with great joy.
He shared the gist of their message with us.
They told us -
- To be a true, faithful disciple of Jesus Christ, even unto death.
- That the coming of Jesus Christ was very near.
- To keep our garments of righteousness white and spotless.
- To prepare ourselves as the Bride for Jesus Christ the Heavenly Bridegroom.
- That they were sealing 144,000 Jewish Virgins in special Service to Jesus Christ.
- That the Signs they were doing demonstrate their Calling and the Power of God.

Isaac said that he felt motivated to finish his assignment for God and encouraged us to do the same.

Moses and Elijah also preached to the world.
There message was about the true Living God Jehovah, His Word, Laws, requirements and righteousness.
They proclaimed that Jesus Christ would soon be crowned King of Kings.
That He would return to the earth to restore it and set up His righteous Kingdom.
People mocked them and out rightly rejected their message.
The world hated and despised them.
They called for their arrest and execution and several attempts were made to kill them.
Then judgment fire went out of the Prophets mouth and consumed them.

Wherever Elijah stretched out his hands over an area it became drought stricken.
When Moses stretched out his hands over the rivers or ocean, it turned to blood.
They were untouchable and couldn't be tracked down or captured.

Then the terrible day came when the Witnesses were preaching in Jerusalem.
Abbadon came up from the bottomless pit and attacked them.
They were killed and their dead bodies were left to lie in front of the Temple.
The world celebrated their death and gave gifts to each other.
After 3½ days the world was shocked to see them resurrected and raptured into Heaven.

Earlier towards the beginning of the tribulation, there were constant strange rumors.
These were reports of UFO's and Alien appearances.
These reports were documented in newspapers and the media.
Many came from reputable sources and could not be discounted.
Then a shocking announcement came.

The World President Mohammad Reza had met with an Alien Leader.
It was reported, that they were going to make a joint global appearance on international television.
The World was told that they were about to sign an important Treaty of global importance.
The next Friday evening, they appeared together sitting at a golden conference table.

First the President took his place at the table.
Then a small strange looking creature, with a large head and large dark glassy eyes appeared.
He was ushered in to sit on the left side of the President.
The President announced that he had agreed to give large amounts of minerals, metals, gold and precious stones to the Alien Nation.
The Alien Leader in turn gave amazing new technologies and information that would dramatically change and help the world.
This ratified agreement immediately opened the door for UFO's and Alien Creatures to appear unobtrusively, all over the world.

The Leader of this Alien Community was invited to speak on television to the World.
He wanted to enlighten the World about the interaction they had had with the World over the past six thousand year period.
These five aspects were given one by one -

First –
He said that Alien appearances over 6000 years of human history were documented by many humans.
He presented the following as corroborating evidence:
- 3000 B.C in India, the texts Bhagavata-Purana, Mahabharata and Ramayana were of UFO's
- Ancient Egyptian legends referred to aliens as "sky gods" that came down to Earth
- Alexander the Great and his Army reported seeing two UFO's.

- So did the Persians, Assyrians, Greeks, Arabs and Roman Armies.
- In China in 420 AD, a book by Gan Bao told of contact with Aliens.
- In 1000 AD the Mayans said they made contact with extraterrestrials called "The Masters of the Stars."
- In England in 1290, Yorkshire Peasants reported spotting UFO's.
- In 1566 residents of Nuremberg, Germany and Basel, Switzerland observed sphere, disc and tube crafts flying in the skies.
- In 1716, Astronomer Edmond Halley observed aerial displays of UFO's.
- In 1878, a Farmer in Dallas, Texas saw a large flying UFO
- On November 17, 1896, flying UFO's were spotted over Sacramento, California.
- That there were many similar 20th century Media Pictures and Reports documented.

As further proof, he projected pictures that people all over the world could view on television.
They were taken by Aliens for their historical record.
It showed pictures of famous people taken during their life on earth.
It also showed important events that took place throughout the 6000 years of world history.
Their's was far more detailed and accurate, than historical records recorded by human historians.
All of this was shocking and indisputable.

Second –
He said that all forms of life were created in evolutionary succession, as a result of Alien scientific experiments.
He also said that the first man and woman, Adam and Eve were created by them.

Third –
He alleged that these Biblical events were actually orchestrated by Aliens:
* Aliens took human wives and had children with them. (Genesis 6:4)
* Aliens helped Moses to part the red sea
* Aliens created the appearance of God to Moses on Mt Sinai
* They caused the destruction of the walls of Jericho
* They destroyed Sodom and Gomorrah
* That Elijah was carried up in a UFO
* That Ezekiel described seeing UFO's – Ezekiel 1:1-28
* That they caused the virgin birth of Jesus

Fourth –
He said that man was in the process of destroying the earth and that was why they intervened to save man and the planet.

Fifth –
He said that in order for man to survive, mankind should serve the Antichrist and be obedient to his Prophet.

So convincing was this message that it was immediately embraced by most people.

THE FALSE PROPHET, TWO WITNESSES AND HORRIFIC TIMES

The greatest tragedy was that it devastated the faith of many Christians.
This was the big lie and falling away that Paul had warned the Christians about. 2 Thessalonians 2:2-11

As Christians we wanted to know more about their origin.
Our information was very limited.
We understood them to be Pre-Edenic Creatures.
They were not created in the image and likeness of God.
They were misled by satan and their Pre-Edenic Earth was destroyed.
With all their advanced technologies they made their abode amongst the stars.
In the tribulation the heavens were being shaken.
Eventually the sun, moon and stars would be destroyed.
They were being forced to come to the Earth and this had far reaching implications.
We found scriptures in the Bible that alluded to this.

People were also influenced by new age and other false teachings.
Many prominent Church Leaders and Evangelists indulged in sinful and questionable practices.
This brought great shock and confusion to weak Christians.

Then came the railing accusation of religious clerics saying –
"Where is this rapture people preached about?
There is no such thing. It is figment of your imagination."

THE APOCALYPSE THEN GLORY

For many it brought their final defeat.
They surrendered to the damnable persuasions of the heretic satanic church.

Chapter Four

The Jewish Temple, persecution and Martyrdom

Two years into the tribulation, the Jewish Temple in Jerusalem was completed and dedicated.

It towered on the East side of the city of Jerusalem at the east gate.
This huge magnificent Temple changed the face of Jerusalem.
The middle structure was rectangular and one hundred feet high.
It was crowned with Gold around the four sides at the top.
At the front was a large exquisitely carved wooden Door.
On each side it had two high gold pillars that glistened in the sun.

In front of the door was a white stone platform.
Twelve white stone steps led down from it to the Temple area below.
It was also paved with white stone.
In front was a ramp, leading to a huge 40 ft square stone altar that was 25 ft high.
Barefooted Priests performed their duties ascending and descending from the Altar.
On this Altar animals were sacrificed each day.
This created a huge column of smoke that ascended straight up into Heaven.

Inside the Temple were Purification Micah Baths.
There the Priests immersed and purified themselves.
Beyond this was the Holy Place that was made of pure white marble.
Inside, on the one side was a Golden Table for showbread.
On the other side was a Golden Candelabrum with seven branches.
In front was a Golden Altar of Incense.
Behind this altar was a thick woven curtain, leading to the Holy of Holies.
It was beautifully woven with finely twisted blue, purple and scarlet yarn.
It had cherubim skillfully worked into it by the best craftsmen.
This magnificent Temple was loved and revered by Jews everywhere!

It was at this time that Jews everywhere began to experience unprecedented persecution.
They were ridiculed for believing in the Torah and practicing the Ten Commandments.

They were attacked and ostracized for practicing animal sacrifices in Jerusalem.
They were criticized for practicing the health and ceremonial laws of the Bible.
They were mocked for their belief in the sanctity of marriage and strong family relationships.

They were prosecuted for circumcising their eight day old male babies.
Genital mutilation laws were passed and many Jews were indicted and imprisoned.
The terrible day arrived when they began to be denied access to public and community places.
They were openly embarrassed for their Jewish heritage.
In many places they were forced to wear identification items, just like in the time of Hitler.
Millions of Jews immigrated back to Israel.
Their enemies planned to isolate them in Israel and then exterminate them there.

The persecution of the Christians followed similar lines.
Laws were passed by the World Government.
They were subtly designed to attack what true Christians believed and practiced.
The persecution grew so intense that we were isolated and denigrated.
We experienced what Christians must have experienced in Biblical times.

Our behavior and lifestyle was vastly different from the rest of the World.
Our thoughts, words, actions and habits were different.

We could not buy or sell because we did not have the mark of the beast.
We could not find employment.
We did not qualify for any health, medical or dental treatment.
We had no access to any community or government aid.
Our children were denied access to schools.

Another dreaded day arrived.
Christians and Jews alike were compelled to receive the Mark of the Beast.
They were told to pledge allegiance to the Antichrist.
They were forced to deny the Faith.
The ultimatum was to obey or be arrested.

The different strategies Authorities applied to locate and arrest unyielding Christians were -
Betrayal
Surveillance and
Bated Traps

They worked their system relentlessly.
Eventually many family members betrayed each other.
Arrest warrants were issued and Officers arrived at residences to arrest helpless Christians. Thousand were whisked away to Detention Centers.
From there black helicopters carried them off to Concentration Camps.
Upon arrival there, they were met with cold, unemotional words -
"Christian or Jew, deny your faith or suffer capital punishment by Guillotine."

THE JEWISH TEMPLE, PERSECUTION AND MARTYRDOM

Many faithfully would not recant their faith.
They were martyred for the Word of God and their testimony.
Some victoriously shouted chants of victory as they were led to the guillotine.
One of the popular chants was –
"Jesus thank you for dying on the Cross for me.
I love you and gladly sacrifice my life for you."

Rivers of Martyr Blood flowed throughout the world.
Some of us were fortunate enough to escape arrest, but were systematically being hunted down. Every method and technology was used in the process and they regarded no cost too high.
Black helicopters continuously scanned over landscapes to find dissidents.

House Churches were declared illegal.
Church services were raided without warning and all participants arrested.
Drones constantly did surveillance over suspect houses.
They used Satelite imaging and military spy technology.
Prosecuting information was collected and pieced together.

Bill, Mary and their Home Church Members, were some of many unfortunate victims.
They were betrayed by a relative of someone who was attending their home church.
Authorities constantly watched their house.
Authorities used Web bugs and Cyber stalking to intercept the messaging between the Christians.

A raid followed and all the participating Christians were arrested.
Most of them became Martyrs for their Faith.

We knew that our communications were being tracked with their tracking software.
Some Christian Itech and Electronic Technicians helped us to counteract that.
We also used intricate, advanced bug tracking devices to avoid detection.

On another occasion we were in flight after narrowly escaping arrest.
We had been going from house church to house church, ministering and encouraging Christians.
A non- believing person in the neighborhood had noticed us coming and going from the house.
She suspected that it was church related and subtlety befriended the Christian Family.
After confirming her suspicions, she notified the authorities and the house was placed under surveillance. One of our informants warned us that we were about to be arrested.

We knew that they would track us with their GPS tracking technology while escaping.
We discarded all our Identification cards.
The radio-frequency identification (RFID) tags in them would be fed into a Homeland Security database.
We were also aware of the fact that they would do Satellite imaging and tracking.
We immediately checked for tracking bugs, magnetically attached under our vehicle.
We found one and removed it.

THE JEWISH TEMPLE, PERSECUTION AND MARTYRDOM

We knew that our arrest was imminent and we immediately packed all necessities and left.
We travelled along back roads, avoiding potential road blocks.

Coming to a dirt road we followed it to a place where we turned off and drove into the bush.
There we concealed the vehicle covering it with branches and leaves.
We removed all scent of our tracks.
We did this by spraying a special scent to confuse tracking dogs.
We knew that they would try to track us.
We always listened for barking dogs that would indicate that they were coming our way.

From there we proceeded many winding miles, to our secret pre-determined location.
We had built a secret, concealed log cabin near to a creek.
We covered it with a heat shielding cover.
This was to avoid thermal detection and imaging from helicopters flying overhead.
Whenever we moved outside the cabin, we also covered ourselves with a heat shielding cover.
We did this when we were foraging, fishing, hunting or getting water.
We lived there for some time and from there we continued to have contact with home church leaders.
There we were also blessed to be able to use intricate devices and avoid detection.
We secretly went and came in Ministry from this location.

Christian Leaders continued to evade the authorities.
They were effective in helping, exhorting and comforting their fellow Christians.
Many were kept in hiding in the homes of Christians but this was not easy.
I remember lying in a trunk of a car, being taken from one secret place to another.
Once I was housed in an underground shelter and had food and water brought to me.
On another occasion several of us camped out in a cave near a stream.
We lived by foraging and catching fish.

There were wonderful highlights that we enjoyed during this time of persecution.
Our secret Home Church Gatherings were a delight.
It was a time of fellowship where we laughed and cried together.
We enjoyed the camaraderie, continuously encouraging each other.

The closed door Prayer gatherings were precious.
Believers would pray and the soft buzzing sound of multiple voices sounded in agreement.
There the warm presence of the Holy Spirit blanketed us and Gods glory was all around us.
We were waiting for the rapture and the great coming of our Heavenly Bridegroom, Jesus Christ.

At least once a month, several families would come together to have Holy Communion.
We ate bread and drank grape juice that was especially stored away for that purpose.
We wanted to remember the death and resurrection of our Lord until he came.

Softly everyone harmonized in beautiful songs –
"He is Lord, He is Lord
and
Oh, how I love Jesus
and
Because He lives I can face tomorrow."

In Ministry
Our main task was to prepare the Bride for Christ their Heavenly Bridegroom.
Two scriptures that formed the basis of our message were -

Titus 2:11-14
"The grace of God that brings salvation hath appeared to all men.
Teaching us that, denying ungodliness and worldly lusts, we should live soberly, righteously, and godly, in this present world;
Looking for that blessed hope, and the glorious appearing of the great God and our Savior Jesus Christ;
Who gave himself for us, that he might redeem us from all iniquity, and purify unto himself a peculiar people, zealous of good works."

Revelation 19:7
"Let us be glad and rejoice, and give honor to him: for the marriage of the Lamb is come, and his wife hath made herself ready."

There were many false doctrines that were preached in the name of God.
We spent much time teaching the Saints the truth of God's Word.

THE APOCALYPSE THEN GLORY

We were ostracized on every hand because we were not a part of the world ecumenical church.
Its teachings had misled so many Christians.
It accommodated *all* religions.
It allowed *false* speaking in tongues, healings and miracles.
It also allowed sinister and dark kinds of belief.
It revered the False Prophet and worshipped the Antichrist and Lucifer who gave him power.

The persecution intensified and there were food and other shortages.
It soon became necessary for us to greatly supplement our food supplies with foraged food.
Fortunately I had taken some time to teach and train others about foraging.
They in turn helped me to take many Christians on foraging trips.
Then it became enjoyable for families to do this together.
They learnt how to find edible mushrooms and wild onions.
They learnt how to pick poke, lambs quarters, shepherds purse, watercress and stinging nettle.
Nuts, berries and wild fruit were added to their foraging baskets.
Some of the others Saints were good at catching fish or hunting.
We did our best to help each other.

Sometimes groceries were acquired from contacts we had.
People who were kindly disposed to us, helped us.
The ladies would come together on baking days to bake bread and cookies.

They became ingenious in finding ways to make different kinds of flour.
On other days they would can vegetables and fruit.
This would be a whole day operation.
At times the men would slaughter an animal and dress it.
There were different cuts of meat.
We would make ground sausage and bratwurst.
We had a special recipe to make dried jerky and it lasted a long time.
This was a treat we enjoyed while travelling and it was a blessing.
Ever so often we slaughtered a hog.
That was well received including the bacon.

We equally shared what we had and took care of each other's needs.
It was very much like in the days of the early Church of Acts.

From time to time we had to help each other with maintenance of vehicles or houses.
There were many acts of love performed every day among unbelievers.
Sometimes it would take a whole day to fix a car or home.
All Christians participated including the Leaders and Pastors.
This touched the hearts of many as they saw genuine deeds of love.

Often a request went out for dental or medical help.
This included extracting teeth, dressing wounds or treating sickness.
We used available natural and pharmaceutical remedies.

Sometimes calls for help were made to Christian Doctors, Dentists, Pharmacists, Nurses and Medical contacts we had.
As time progressed it became more and more difficult.

One of our major tasks was taking care of Orphaned Children who had lost their parents.
We had to hide them from the authorities and place them with foster Christian Parents.
They would care for them and protect them.
That prevented the authorities from taking and placing them with unbelieving Foster Parents.
These would indoctrinate them to deny their faith.
Often Widows and Single Parents needed our help.
Helping the needy was a part of our everyday routine.

Another important task that we emphasized was the education of the children.
We encouraged Parents to be vitally involved in teaching them.
Even in the time of the tribulation, it was necessary to teach our children how to read and write.
Their textbook was the Bible.
They were taught spelling, math, science, computer science and other subjects at home school.
Many Parents who had done this in the past gave guidance.

Experiencing disaster
We were awakened one morning to devastating news on national television.
A massive earthquake had devastated the City of London.

Most of the important historic buildings such as Buckingham Palace, Windsor Castle, Westminster Abbey, Big Ben were totally crumbled to rubble and ruined.
People fled to the neighboring cities and towns for help and shelter.
This earthquake was followed by aftershocks in rapid succession for days.

Then another major 9.5 earthquake shook the Netherlands and it was horrific.
Most cities and towns were destroyed.
The Dykes collapsed and the ocean that was held back for so many years flooded the land.
It was like a major Tsunami.
Millions of lives were lost.
People were homeless living in tents and shelters.

It was evident that this was caused by major continental shifts.
The crust of the earth seemed to be cracking open.
The whole world was in shock because of the close succession of these events.
Many did not realize that these were nature's birth pains.
They would bring forth the birth of the Glorious New World of Jesus Christ the Messiah.
If that wasn't enough, another catastrophe followed two months later.
There was a volcanic eruption of unprecedented magnitude.
It was one of the greatest eruptions of all time.
It came without a warning in the Canary Islands, on the island of La Palma.

THE APOCALYPSE THEN GLORY

The volcano of Cumbre Vieja erupted and sent a massive side of a mountain crashing into the ocean.
A giant 300 ft high tsunami travelled across 4,000 miles of the Atlantic.
Within 6 hours it hit the Caribbean islands and the east coasts of the United States and Canada.
A devastating 100 feet Tsunami pounded the coastline and wiped out everything in its way.
Major Cities and population areas on America's East Coast were obliterated within minutes.
Hundreds of millions of people were killed in the Cities including New York.
It stretched inland for up to 25 miles toward Washington, destroying everything in its path.
Thousands of cargo ships, oil tankers and Navy ships were destroyed.
The world was thrust into hopelessness and total despair.

In the past treacherous plagues had afflicted the World.
Suddenly new plagues began to manifest everywhere.
They were widespread, infectious, terrible and fast spreading.
There was no time to create effective antibiotics or treatments.
They were flesh eating, internal organ destroying, blood poisoning and body debilitating plagues.
People sealed themselves in their homes to protect themselves.
Others moved away to remote locations to avoid human contact and infection.
Once again we saw scripture being fulfilled before our eyes.

Revelation 9:20

"And the rest of the men which were not killed by these plagues yet repented not of the works of their hands, that they should not worship devils and idols."
One Saturday afternoon at about 3 pm a large Meteorite burst through the atmosphere lighting up the sky. The brilliance of its light was like a thousand Suns.
It fell burning its way into the Atlantic Ocean off the coast of Spain.
The tidal wave it caused was devastating, hitting that part of the coast of Europe.
Immediately it affected a third part of the ocean, clouds and rivers and they became bitter and poisonous. Many people and animals died as a result of drinking water.
It also caused partial darkness, inhibiting the light of the sun to shine through.
A third part of the sun, a third part of the moon and a third part of the stars were darkened.

The Saints of God remained Strong in the Lord and fearless.
Our favorite scripture was -

Psalm 46:1-2

"God is our refuge and strength, a very present help in trouble. Therefore will not we fear, though the earth be removed, and though the mountains be carried into the midst of the sea;"

It was at that time that the Antichrist made an announcement.
He was bringing together the most brilliant scientists of the World.

Within days they had an emergency meeting in Babylon.
This meeting was teleconferenced to all the leading Scientific Centers in the world.
All of the world's top scientists participated and had privy to the information that was shared.
The following dangers were discussed:
- The tilting of the earth as a result of meteorite impact with the earth.
- The catastrophic climate change that had taken place
- The rising sea level causing geographical changes
- The effects of the residual meteorite material left behind in the ocean
- Dying sea and plant life
- Increased overheating of the sun and the threat of it possibly burning out
- The shifting of the continent plates and immanent killer earthquakes

They had tried to ignore the fulfillment of the prophecies and warnings of the Bible.
Now they were forced to come to the realization of what they were experiencing.
It was Gods Apocalyptic Judgment upon the Earth.
Many sought refuge in mountain caves.
Some built underground shelters.
The more affluent moved into underground communities.
Fear was gripping humanity for the things that were coming upon the world.

Then an unbelievable report came.

THE JEWISH TEMPLE, PERSECUTION AND MARTYRDOM

Millions of strange creatures were appearing all over the world attacking people.
So great was the cry of people who were suffering, in pain and desperation.
They were facing a merciless satanic enemy that had come from the bottomless pit, to torment them.
It was Abaddon who led this evil army and he only inflicted those who had the Mark of the Beast.
The world was helpless!

This fitted a description found in the Bible – Revelation 9:4, 16-21
We understood the Prophecies of the Bible, knew what was happening and what would follow.
Seven vials were being poured out by the seven Angels.
Grievous sores would inflict the bodies of people.
It was suggested that the computer chip implants would be the cause of that.
The rising heat of a sun, seven times hotter, would scorch men like fire.
There would be 100 pound size hailstones that would devastate all of the earth.
A gross darkness would follow, so intense that people would gnaw their tongues in agony.

It became most unbearable for the Christians who were still alive.
The Holy Spirit comforted us and we cried out to God.
Our desperate cry reached Heaven –
Come quickly Lord Jesus!

Part Two

Chapter Five

Heaven bound

Suddenly there was an unexpected, strong shout of a word –
It was COME!
It echoed through the Heavens and all the Christians clearly heard it.
It was quickly followed by a heralding Trumpet sound.
It was the wonderful sound of the 7th Trumpet we were waiting for.
It was the Rapture call.

The Biblical promise of the Coming of Christ for His Church was being fulfilled -
"We shall all be changed, In a moment, in the twinkling of an eye, at the last trump:
For the trumpet shall sound, and the dead shall be raised incorruptible, and we shall be changed.
For the Lord himself shall descend from heaven with a shout, with the voice of the archangel

and with the trump of God: and the dead in Christ shall rise first:
Then we which are alive and remain shall be caught up together with them in the clouds, to meet the Lord in the air: and so shall we ever be with the Lord."

Suddenly I was caught up through the blue sky.
I was being translated through the atmosphere.
I was rapidly travelling upwards toward a Great Light.
I saw millions of Saints coming together from all directions.
In the bright light above us, Jesus appeared in magnificence and glory.

I arrived at the indescribable Paradise of Heaven.
My full attention now became focused on where I was.
I covered my face with my hands, to shield my eyes.
My eyes were getting accustomed to the glorious light ahead of me.
I continued walking along a path with beautiful plants and trees on either side.
Then I found myself approaching a large crowd of people all clothed in pure white linen.

I turned to my right and there was a large Angel walking beside me.
He spoke to me and said -
"I am your guardian Angel and I have been with you your whole life.
These people have been waiting for you. Go ahead toward them and meet them."

As I got close, suddenly a young lady burst from the crowd, ran, embraced and kissed me.
She said - "I am your daughter Marie – welcome to Heaven."
Then she gestured to the crowd and oh what a sight.
There were my parents, my in-laws and my Family.

I saw my two Sisters whom I had never met and they came and hugged me.
My grandparents and other extended family members were there and I embraced them one by one.
As I looked over the rest of the crowd behind them, I began to recognize them.
I saw Saints who I had led to the Lord.
There were those who I had shepherded while Pastoring Churches.
I recognized many of my Christian friends.
I also saw several Spiritual mentors who had played a major part in my Spiritual Life and Ministry.
Some were Ministry Colleagues who had labored with me for the Lord.
The list goes on and on and I was so happy to see them all.

Then there was a hush and a silence in the crowd.
I smelt the most wonderful fragrance like that of a rose.
The crowd graciously parted, and there stood the One who I had waited so long to meet.
It was my Lord and Savior Jesus Christ.
He stood there in all His majesty and Glory and smiled at me.

I ran and fell at His feet. I cried for joy and then I felt Him touch my shoulder, He said -
"Arise My child."
I stood and looked into His face. He showed me His hands and I saw the nail scars.
He said -
"I did it for you."
Again I fell at His feet.
I was breathless and couldn't speak.
Again He touched me and strength entered into me.
I cried and with many tears I said -
"Thank you Jesus."

Then He lifted me up by the hand and said -
"Well done my good and faithful servant. Enter into the joy of your Lord."
I looked past Him and there was Heaven in all its Glory.
Oh what a wonderful sight!

For a moment I was lost in the ecstasy of it all, and then the Angel said to me –
"In Heaven there are no limitations or earthly dimensions and time.
All who were raptured are being met and welcomed just like you.
There is something uniquely special, for each of them.
Now come with me and see what the Lord has prepared for you."

I looked at myself and at my new body.
It is about the same size as my earthly body.
It is made of spirit material, cloud-like, semitransparent, opaque and glowing.

My garment that covered me is the most beautiful I had ever seen.
It is a single pure white garment of the finest soft linen.

Movement
Body movements of standing, walking, sitting and dancing are very much the same in Heaven.
There is however one significant difference.
At the speed of thought, one can effortlessly travel any distance within the allowed estate.
Each glorified body has its own unique fragrance.
Jesus has a most amazing fragrance like that of a rose.
Whenever he is nearby one knows of His presence.
Gestures such as smiles, hugs, kisses are very normal in Heaven.

Then the Angel said that it was time for me to approach the Throne of God.
There was this thick, partially transparent veil that reached high into Heaven.
It separated the Throne of God from the rest of Heaven.
We approached this glory veil and passed through it.
I experienced the most wonderful satisfying, warm, exhilarating, purifying feeling.
I then stood looking at a sea of glass before me that stretched far into the distance.
I saw at the end of it the Throne of God.
It was high, wide and immeasurable.
It reached into eternity.
Upon it sat -
The Most High God.
The Ancient of Days.

The Almighty Jehovah.

His presence filled eternity and Heaven.
This presence of pure translucent mists of gold flowed to and through everything.
It discerned -
Feelings
Thoughts
Motives
Decisions
Tastes
Desires
Communications
Conversations
Activities
Everything

Things that are good, pure and holy bring pleasure to Him.

Then there were countless lightning's that proceeded from Gods Throne.
They passed through Heaven, the Universe and Eternity.
I was told that they are the Decrees of God, effecting and upholding all things.
They are also God's answers to prayer.

Beyond the sea of glass were terraces that led up to this immeasurable Throne.
It took time for my eyes to adjust to the brightness and brilliance of God's presence.
Eventually I could see the outline of an awesome Being.
On His right side was another Person.

They were both covered in the brightest light I had ever seen.
It was too bright to continuously look upon.
Multi colored beams of light shone from Them, passing through everything and Heaven.
Around the Throne was an emerald colored rainbow of Glory.
Large Creatures were on either side of the Throne.
In front of the Throne at a lower level were 7 burning Lamps.
In front of the Lamps was a huge Golden Altar that was inscribed with the words -
"The prayers of the Saints."

Two Angels stood on either side with golden censors in their hands.
Out of the censors they poured incense on the altar.
The incense was the Prayers of the Saints that had been stored away. Revelation 8:3

At a lower level on either side were twelve seats.
Upon them sat twenty four Elders.
Twelve represented the Old Testament Saints and twelve the New Testament Saints.
I was speechless.
I was in Heaven, before Gods Eternal Throne.

I found myself laying prostrate before God my Heavenly Father.
I felt that deep sense of belonging, security, rest and peace at my Fathers feet.
I was thankful for my eternal relationship with Him.
This was the culmination of my highest hopes and dreams.

THE APOCALYPSE THEN GLORY

On earth I had prayed to God and He heard and answered my prayers.
When I sinned I asked for His forgiveness.
He always forgave me and cleansed me with the precious Blood of Jesus.
He lovingly extended His grace toward me and gave me favor.
He blessed me with my wonderful wife Marie.
He gave us two children Mark and Charlene.
Then He blessed us with Dale Sikkema and my grandchildren Dale, Isaac and Eden.
He provided all my needs and most desires.

He granted me the privilege to work for Him and equipped me to do His work.
I learnt to privately go into His presence.
I sang songs to Him and He gave me new songs to sing.
I was privileged on earth to always express my thanks to Him for all His goodness to me.
He allowed me to give Him praise for who He is.
I always cherished those moments.
I was allowed into His presence and there next to my bed I worshipped Him.
There I felt His warm presence and it was awesome.
I knew that I was in my Fathers hands, and no-one could snatch me out of them – John 10:29

Now that I was in Heaven I had eternity ahead of me.
I looked with great anticipation to my continued relationship with my Heavenly Father.
I knew that He would tell me what He wanted me to do and what His desires were for me.

I was looking forward to experience the things that He had prepared for me.
"But as it is written, Eye hath not seen, nor ear heard, neither have entered into the heart of man, the things which God hath prepared for them that love him." 1 Corinthians 2:9.

Then God spoke to me -
His great voice penetrated my entire being.
His voice sounded like that of many waters.
It resonated with depth, strength and power.
It gave me the overwhelming assurance and security that I needed from a Father.

He knew everything about me.
He gave me all the reasons why.
He surprised me with all the wonderful blessings He had in store for me.
He assured me that soon I would be a part of the Marriage of His Son Jesus.
He said that there were special things that Jesus had planned for me to do in His Kingdom.
My whole being vibrated as He spoke to me.

Jesus
It was an amazing sight to see Jesus sitting at the right hand of God.
God the Father had seated Him there after his ascension into Heaven.
Electrifying Power, Strength and Glory proceeded from him.
Just one glimpse of Him, brought me prostrate upon my face.
Without his help, I could never survive it.

When He spoke it was like deep sounding, roaring waters.
Every word was crisp and clear.
When that happened, myriads of Angels fell on their faces and worshipped Him.
I was thankful that I belonged to Him and felt cared for and secure in His presence.

It was wonderful to be a part of the great multitude of Blood washed Saints.
We would all fall down before Him and say -
"You are worthy oh Lord. You were slain and have redeemed us to God by your blood.
Lamb of God, You are worthy to receive power, riches, wisdom, strength, honor, glory and blessing."

The Holy Spirit
Heaven had become the home of multitudes of Saints.
They were the Spirits of just men made perfect and I was one of them. Hebrews 12:23
When on earth, we were baptized with the Holy Spirit.
We were made one with Him and sealed by God.
We lived and walked in the Spirit.
Now that we were in Heaven our spirit remained joined to the Holy Spirit.
His seal was still upon us.
His presence in us connected us to Jesus and God the Father in a miraculous and glorious way. We were part of Gods Family.
His Divine Nature was a part of our new glorified being.
It enabled us to do what was required in excellence, pleasing God.

It was at this time that Jesus spoke to the Angel and said -
"Show him all the glories of Heaven and his Heavenly Mansion."

Chapter Six

Heaven

We passed back through the transparent thick glorious veil that reached high, into the Heavens. Walking westward down a wide transparent golden highway, we passed through the middle of the City. The highway was large enough for millions of people to walk on at the same time.

I looked back toward the veil again.
In front of it are two Reserved Areas.
On the one side of the street, is a large area.
It is the reception area where the **Raptured Saints** were first received into Heaven.

On the other side of the street are two other areas.
In the one area is a huge High Altar with a large place of waiting below.
There millions of **Martyrs** find themselves.
These are they who had shed their blood as Martyrs for their Faith.
It was their sacrifice and it was pleasing to God.

Romans 12:21. Revelation 15:2. Revelation 7:14-15
Whenever called, they would stand on the Sea of Glass before Gods Throne.
Then they would play their Harps and sing songs of worship to God.

The other area is for the **144.000 Virgins of Christ.**
When called, they would also go beyond the veil and stand on the Sea of Glass.
They would play their Harps and sing the songs of Moses and of the Lamb.
Revelation 14:1-3

The Temple in Heaven.
As I proceeded I saw a towering structure.
It was huge, magnificent, beyond description.
The smoke of Shekinah Glory and the Power of God filled it and ascended into Heaven from it.
The Angel told me that the Ark of the Covenant was kept in it. Revelation 9:19

He said that the Temple had a Heavenly High Priest, whose name was Melchisedek.
His work is to oversee the service, functions and activities of the Temple.
All the Heavenly Priests are appointed after His order.
They do seven important tasks:
1. When called upon, they sound the Trumpets, heralding the commencement of events.
2. They pour out vials and the Golden vial, which contains the incense of the Saints prayers.
3. They work as scribes recording information that God wants recorded.

4. They summon and direct praise and worship.
   - They signal Orchestras to play.
   - They signal Choirs to sing.
   - They signal Halutzim dancing and celebrations of joy in Heaven.
5. They perform Priestly services on behalf of the Saints.
6. They perform ceremonial functions on Heavenly High Days.
7. They provide Teaching Service in Heaven.

The Angel said that when Jesus was resurrected from the dead, He immediately entered the Temple in Heaven.
God the father then appointed Him a High Priest forever, after the order of Melchisidek.
He went beyond the veil into the Holy of Holies
There He sprinkled His precious Blood as an eternal offering for the sins of all of mankind.

I asked the **Angel** to tell me more about **the Angels.**
He said that Angels are different in rank and size.
That God has assigned them many different responsibilities.
I saw them coming in and out of the Temple, performing different duties.
They appeared in dazzling white and with blazing glory.
I remembered reading in Luke 2 of the shepherds in the field.
They saw Angels and the glory of the Lord shining all around, and were "sore afraid."

Some Angels I saw were holding Golden Vials, some carrying Books and Scrolls.

Some proceeded to the Throne of God for special instructions.
Others left on special assignments.
Some of the Angels I was told, were taking special care of Orphan children on earth.
(I knew that God said that He is a Father to Orphans.)
However I was also told that the supreme activity of Angels is to worship and praise God.

I knew that some served as Messengers of God to communicate with men.
There were many, moving between Heaven and Earth.
Examples of this is found in the Bible.
- Special messages were given by an Angel to Gideon and Daniel.
- Joseph of Mary, Philip and Cornelius were given special instructions by Angels.
- An Angel was used by God to provide food for Hagar and Elijah.
- An Angel protected Daniel in the lion's den and his three friends in the fiery furnace.
- An Angel stirred the waters at the Pool of Bethesda, bringing healing to the sick.
- An Angel delivered Peter from prison.
- Angels brought strength and encouragement to Jesus in Gethsemane.
- An Angel stood by Paul before he was shipwrecked.

Both my wife and others I know have experienced Angelic encounters on earth.

The Bible teaches that they are Ministering Spirits sent to serve the Saints.
Hebrews 1:14

I proceeded and then noticed another towering structure.
I was told that it is the **Supreme, Eternal Court of Heaven.**
All the Books of Heaven are kept in it.

Several books of great importance are there:
The Book of Life
In this Book is written the names of all who are Children of the Most High God.

The Book of the War's of the Lord
In it the names and stories of Saints who have been in battle for the Lord, are recorded.
This book was to be opened and read at the Bema Seat of Christ.

The Book of seven seals that was opened by Jesus. Revelation 4.
First this book was spoken of by many who wanted to know what was written in it.
They were amazed because they could not open it.
Then it was taken to God on His Throne, who gave it to Jesus.
He broke open the seals and revealed the contents.
This had happened at the beginning of the seven year tribulation. Revelation 5:5. 6:1

There is also a Book about every Person or Creature that has ever lived.
Each book contains every detail of a person's life.

All their thoughts, actions, words, and feelings are recorded.
I was told that my book was there as well.
King David referred to this book.
"Thou tellest my wanderings: are they not in thy book?" Psalm 56:8

There was a Book of the Historical Record of all time.
In this book, every detail of everything that happened throughout time is recorded.

The Angel also mentioned that these books would be used at the White Throne Judgment of God.
Just like all other Courts, this Heavenly Court has Judicial Activities.
The proceedings are very similar.
The accuser is satan.
The Righteous Advocate is Jesus Christ.
The Judge is God.
At times satan would appear to accuse the Saints of their sins and failures in their absence.
Then Jesus would advocate on their behalf and defense before God.
Books would be brought and used as evidence in our favor.
However this had changed at the time of our rapture into Heaven.
It was at this time that satan was expelled and cast out of Heaven onto the Earth,
He never would enter Heaven again and be allowed to accuse any Christian. Rev 12:10

Throughout the City there were many **spectacular buildings**.

They were different sizes and architectural styles and were -
- Banquet halls used for Festivals and Reunions.
- Amphitheaters featuring notable Saints.
- Celebration Centers used to hold great Feasts.

The enjoyment of Food and drink is an important aspect of life in Heaven.

There is an abundance of food.
Everything that one desired was available and there were no limitations or shortages.
Whenever people ate, they were satisfied and never overindulged.
There never was a possibility or thought of experiencing lack.
We patiently enjoyed what was set before us and gladly shared what we had with each other.
Eating was part of a higher Heavenly culture.
In excellence we also showed respect to our heavenly bodies and to each other.

A great variety
When on Earth, I had travelled to many countries.
I was introduced to many kinds of indigenous and exotic fruits, vegetables and foods.
How surprised I was in Heaven to continuously discover new varieties.
Every taste I had was satisfied.
Everything I could dream of was available.
One would often hear someone ask -
"Have you tasted this? Here try this."

Tasteful drinks

I knew that on earth connoisseurs tasted and
relished different kinds of drinks.
They knew which grape varieties and harvests
produced the best Wine products.
Vintage Champagnes, White wines and Red wines
had a place on many festive tables.

The Heavenly Wines by far surpass anything ever
produced on earth.
The banqueting tables always display the best of
Heaven and are enjoyed by all.
We would slowly sip and savor the delicious rich
tastes.
Some are velvety and others are clear and crisp.
They vary in color and are delightful.

In Heaven food never dominates a celebration.
It always accentuates the occasion.
It also serves to be symbolical -
- Bread and grain foods celebrate the eternal *Word of God*.
- Fruits celebrate the *Works of God.*
- Foods celebrate the *Teachings of God.*

I experienced something amazing in Heaven.
What I ate and drank had a refreshing and spiritual
effect on me.
It caused my glorious Heavenly Body to glow and
emanate life.
It also had a stimulating effect upon my Divine
Nature.
The love, joy, peace, patience, gentleness,
faithfulness and humility in me were amplified.

On very special occasions, we would be invited to a great Passover Celebration.
Our Lord Jesus would sit at the head table with His twelve Apostles.
Countless millions of us were seated at our designated tables.
Jesus broke Bread and poured out the Wine in a large Cup.
It symbolized His Death, Resurrection and eternal Victory over satan and his kingdom.
We all who had been served ate the bread with Him.
It had a slight sweet honey like taste and melted in my mouth as I ate it.

Then we all stood taking and raising our cups of wine.
Millions of Saints spontaneously shouted a great thunderous shout -
L'chaim –"To Jesus the life."
It was followed by a roaring cheer.
We drank the wine and sat down.
We then all participated in the meal.

The Heavenly culture
On earth my thoughts and actions were often carnal.
However the Holy Spirit brought about a change in me.
He enabled us to partake of God's Divine Nature.
2 Peter 1:4
Now that I was in Heaven, my Heavenly Being was so different.
My thoughts were clean, crisp and clear.
I experienced no intellectual limitations or disabilities.

THE APOCALYPSE THEN GLORY

What I heard, I clearly understood and processed.
I was not subjected to negative influences, impulses and memories.
I was a part of a much higher order of culture.

In Heaven everything is true, just, pure, honest, lovely, good, praiseworthy and Godly.
Everything about me permeated with love and faith.
I was not negatively affected by doubt, mistrust, fear, disappointments, inferiority and pain.
All the Saints, Angels and Heavenly Creatures are forever a part of the same winning team.
There is no competition, only heavenly bliss.

On earth, we had all been subjected to the abuse and attacks of satan and his kingdom.
The damage and contamination wrought to our body, mind, emotions and will, has been removed.
It is gone forever and we love, respect and value each other.

Our Actions reflect the quality of our Divine Nature.
We speak with calmness and confidence.
The sound of every voice is unique and enjoyable.
Words flow fluently and it is easy to express our thoughts.
My mental capacities and abilities are unlimited.
All my conversation and actions are wholesome, up building and fruitful.

Amazingly there are no garbage or waste materials in Heaven.
Everything is good and wholesome.
Foods eaten or things unused immediately de-materialize and harmonize with Heaven.

Colors, sounds and reflections are synchronized to change in perfect harmony.
Their variations are beyond comprehension.
They gently merge into each other.
I was introduced to many new colors and pitches of sound in Heaven.

Mansions

On the outskirts of the City, the Angel pointed out a vast area stretching as far as the eye can see.
It has countless number of Mansions, the beauty for which words fail me.
Everyone is uniquely different and indescribable.
These are the homes of the Saints in Heaven.
Later before returning to the earth, I would enter my home in the New Jerusalem.

My Mansion had a large entrance hall.
Its floor was of inlaid mosaic patterns of colorful flowers.
They were magnificently designed.
It led to a large room with beautiful furnishings.
On the one side were sofa's and couches that were very comfortable and of a soft pink, bisque color.
There was a large table and chairs for dining on the other side.
The table was most exquisitely carved out of a dark precious wood.
It seemed that everything in my home was specifically created with my personal tastes in mind.
The walls were of translucent gold and it had a beige marble floor.
It presented a very peaceful and calm atmosphere.
In my home was a special closet room for all my special garments.

THE APOCALYPSE THEN GLORY

These were for the different feasts, celebrations, and events.
A door led out to a garden that had white marble columns all around it.
It had the greenest grass and colorful, fragrant flower gardens.
There were also luscious fruit trees covered with fruit.

I loved to welcome and receive Guests.
They would include Loved Ones and Saints.
I was told that on a most special occasion, Jesus himself would visit and dine at my home.

The City has streets that are broad and made of translucent gold.
They are thronged with people coming and going, enjoying their wonderful new life.
As I enjoyed my walk, I noticed four people walking, talking and laughing as they went.
They were Pastor Friends who had been with me in Ministry on Earth.
I called out to them and they turned around.
We embraced each other and sat down in a fellowship area nearby.
There we enjoyed reminiscing and talking about Heaven.

There are beautiful gardens and fellowship areas everywhere.
The street I continued walking on led to a Community Gathering Place.
There I saw three Saints in the midst of a happy crowd.

HEAVEN

The Angel told me that they were Lazarus, Mary and Martha the friends of Jesus.

Then I came to a large pearl gate leading out of the city.
Standing at the gate on either side, were two Angels and they were about 10 feet tall.
They smiled at me and ushered me to pass through.
I found myself walking on a wide trail with green grass meadows on either side.
It led to a large open area surrounded by all kinds of trees.
There I found people singing and dancing and many children were playing.
They noticed me, smiled and waved at me.
I smiled and waved back.
There shouts and laughter were echoing everywhere.
The Angel explained to me who the children were that I saw.
They were the unwanted, premature or aborted babies of earthly mothers.
God the Father adopted them into Heaven as His children.

As far as my eyes could see, I was surrounded by lots of mountains and lush, gorgeous valleys.
Far to the horizon I saw a blue mountain range with a colorful skyline.
Winding down the mountains into the valleys, were many gently flowing streams.
Along the banks, the grass was green and there were many trees.
The trees were small and large with different shades of green leaves.

Some had great boughs that reached in all directions.
Amidst the leaves were birds singing their beautiful songs.
Fluttering around were butterflies of all descriptions.
Nestled amongst the trees and bushes were many kinds of animals.
I knew that there were many new exciting discoveries in Heaven awaiting me.
I was looking forward to them.

What was so fascinating about Heaven was the absence of bad things I didn't find there.
There is no suffering
There is no crying
There is no aging
There are no painful diseases
There are no deformities
There is no obesity or addiction
There is no hunger
There is no embarrassment
There is no profanity
There is no jealousy
There is no gossip
There is no harassment
There is no betrayal
There is no crime
There is no uncleanness
There is no contamination

Heaven is a wonderful place and I was glad to be there.
The coronation day arrived for the Crowning of Jesus Christ.

HEAVEN

At first several Angels took their place beyond the Veil on the glassy sea, before the Throne.
They were of high rank and participated in the Coronation.

On the left and the right side huge Orchestras began to play Heavenly Music.
It was melodious, it was delightful and one wished it would never end.
Behind them, millions of Angels were forming a perfect formation.
They formed thousands of blocks and each block had thousands of Angels.
When completed, they formed a semi-circle facing the Throne.
An opening was left in the Middle through which millions of Saints entered, onto the glass sea.
They covered a vast area in glimmering white.
There was great expectation and excitement in the air.

The Throne Room was set.
God the Father sat on His Throne.
Jesus Christ sat beside Him.
The Holy Spirit was manifest as Seven Lamps before Gods Throne.

Then many Crowns were brought in and placed on a Golden Table.
They fitted into each other and formed one High Crown.
Each Crown represented the many aspects of the Life of Jesus namely:
His Person,
His Rewards,

His Honor and
His Domain and Kingship.

God the Father spoke.
With a deep voice that filled all of Heaven, God spoke and said -
"My Son, Your Throne is an eternal one.
The scepter with which you will reign is righteousness."
Hebrews 1:8

Jesus came and stood in front of God the Father.
He was clothed in a White Robe with a purple Sash.
One of the Angels of High Rank stood next to the golden table.
Taking the Crown He set it before God the Father.
The Father then placed the crown on the head of Jesus, speaking personal words to Him.
Then God gave a final Proclamation –
"I crown you King of Kings and Lord of Lords."
This event was so Spectacular and Holy, I wished it would never end.

The Billions of Saints and the Angelic Hosts fell on their faces before Jesus.
We lay there and worshipped our Lord.
Eventually we all stood up and with spontaneous praise shouted -
"We see Jesus, crowned with glory and honor.
The kingdoms of this world are become the kingdoms of our Lord, and of his Christ;
and He shall reign forever and ever."

HEAVEN

Jesus stood there in all Power, Might and Glory.
His eyes were as a flame of fire.
On his head were many crowns.

There was great cheering, singing and dancing that continued on and on.
It is important to understand that time is irrelevant in eternity.
Everything brings great joy and unending happiness.
Nothing is boring or tiresome.
Events continue until their completion.

It was then announced by the Archangel Michael, that Jesus would ascend the Bema.

Jesus then ascended the Bema and sat on a huge white marble seat.
Steps led up to where the Bema was.
It was situated in the middle of a huge high white marble platform overlooking the sea of glass.
Behind it were endless galleries filled with Crowns.
The reflection of the glistening gold and sparkling jewels, created a breathtaking background.

This day of appearing before Christ had arrived when Christians would receive their rewards.
I remember the words of Paul the Apostle -
"For we must all appear before the judgment seat of Christ; that every one may receive the things done in his body, according to that he hath done, whether it be good or bad."
2 Corinthians 5:10

It was our time of Heavenly Graduation.
One by one we came to stand before Christ.

There would not be a Valedictorian.
There would however be those who qualified for Much Greater Rewards.
We looked with interest and wonder as each achiever stood before Jesus.
Again one must remember that there are no time limitations in Heaven.
Every Christian would stand before the Lord and enjoy the fullness of the experience.
It was a special moment that we had looked forward to.
It was a personal moment with Jesus, to be revered forever.

As we stood before the Lord several things happened.

First there was the Purification
We experienced what Paul had spoken of -
"Every man's work shall be made manifest: for the day shall declare it.
The fire shall try every man's work of what sort it is.
If any man's work abide which he hath built thereupon, he shall receive a reward."
1 Corinthians 3:13-14

In a moment of time, every deed I had ever done as a Christian flashed before me.

Some made me feel sad and ashamed and others made me feel glad.
Suddenly a fire from the Lords presence consumed the worthless works and only the good remained.

These good works took on the form of gold, silver, precious stones and were displayed for all to see. This treasure was taken up to a special place of keeping.

Then the Jesus turned to me -
He spoke words of special Recognition
You have been faithful in overcoming.
The He turned to God the Father and said –
I confess his name as an Overcomer before you My Father and all the Angels of Heaven.
Further, I present him faultless before the presence of your Glory with exceeding joy.
Revelation 3:5, Jude 24
How can I describe the joy and excitement I was experiencing?
It felt like an unending dream.

Then I bowed on my knees before the Lord -
The crowning took place.
He placed upon my head Crowns.

There are six crowns one can receive and they are -
1. The Incorruptible Crown
 1 Corinthians 9:25-27
2. The Crown of Life
 Revelation 2:10
3. The Crown of Glory
 1 Peter 5:4
4. The Crown of Righteousness
 2 Timothy 4:8
5. The Crown of Rejoicing
 1 Thessalonians 2:19-20
6. The Soul winners Crown
 Philippians 4:1

Many Saints were appointed as Kings unto the King of Kings Jesus Christ.
We were told that our crowns would appear on our head whenever we performed Kingly duties.
Those who received more than one crown would have different crowns manifesting at different times.
We knew that this would be a wonderful time performing these Royal assignments .
We were destined to serve in the Millennial Kingdom of Jesus Christ.

And so another Chapter in the eternal purposes of God had been fulfilled.

Chapter Seven

The Marriage of the Lamb

When Jesus was on Earth, He promised that God His Father was preparing His Wedding.
Matthew 22:2-8

It is described as the greatest wedding and festive occasion of all time.
It was held before the Throne of God.
The Angelic Hosts surrounded the Holy Place to witnesses this majestic event.

The Bride was made up of countless millions of Saints. For two thousand years she had made herself ready. She had been clothed in pure, fine, white garments of righteousness.

Isaiah prophesied these words of the Bridegroom and the Bride -

"God hath clothed me with the garments of salvation,
He hath covered me with the robe of righteousness,
As a bridegroom decketh himself with ornaments, and as a bride adorneth herself with her jewels."
Isaiah 61:10.

The Bride made her entrance and formed a large circle before Gods Throne.
This processional took a long time.
Finally the millions of Saints were in place.
Suddenly 144.000 of the Bridegroom Virgins appeared singing and dancing.
They led the Bridegroom to where the Bride was.
They sang Solomon's song of the Bridegroom -

"Thy love is better than wine.
Thy name is as ointment poured forth.
Therefore do the virgins love Thee.
We will run after thee:
The King will bring His Bride into his chambers and will be glad and rejoice in Him.
His love will be remembered more than wine:
They that are upright love thee.
Jesus is the rose of Sharon and the lily of the valleys.
As the apple tree among the trees of the wood, so is He among the sons.
There is great delight under his shadow for his fruit is sweet to taste.
He will bring His Bride to the banqueting house.
His banner over her is love."

Then Jesus Christ the Bridegroom appeared and proceeded to the center of the circle of the Bride.

He wore a **Kittel** which is a traditional white Marriage Robe.
It accentuated His Royalty and Holiness.

Then Gabriel the Archangel spoke and said -
"Let us be glad and rejoice for the marriage of the Lamb is come and his Wife hath made herself ready."
Revelation 19:7-9.

The Bride then bowed before the Bridegroom seven times.

The Angelic Orchestras began to play.
Then the Angel Choirs joined in with singing.
They sang the Wedding Song with these words -

"The virgin Bride is the Church of Jesus Christ.
She took her lamp and trimmed it.
Then she took oil in her vessel.
She waited for the Bridegroom to come.
At the sound of the Trumpet there was a cry.
Behold, the bridegroom cometh; go out to meet him.
When He called she went forth to meet the Him.
She was ready and has come to this marriage.
The Bridegroom is Jesus of Nazareth.
He is ready to take His Bride.
The doors to this marriage have been shut."

Following that, the **Ketubah** was presented to Jesus by Gabriel the Archangel.
It is the Marriage Contract that Jesus gave to His Bride.

Jesus took it and read these words from the Ketubah -

"In the presence of Almighty God
I Jesus Christ the Heavenly Bridegroom commit these words to my Heavenly Bride.
Be my wife according to the statutes of Moses, Israel and the true Living God.
I will faithfully support and provide for you as is the custom of all Jewish men.
I will provide an eternal Home for you.
We shall be one in Perfect Union.
I bestow upon you treasures, jewelry, clothing and everything you may ever desire.
I make you a joint Heir of everything I have.
I promise this in accordance with the decrees by our Sages, of blessed memory.
From this moment, this Ketubah shall be valid and binding.
I have paid for it with my Precious Blood I shed on Calvary."

Then He handed it back to Gabriel who set it back on the Table again.
Jesus proceeded to talk and said –
"When I was on Earth I made my final journey to Jerusalem.
I knew that I was destined to be crucified.
However, I had counted the cost.
God My Father You told me that it would be the price I would have to pay.
In return for the great Sacrifice of My Life, I would receive a beautiful Bride.
Here I stand today to receive My Bride.
Father, I give you thanks and praise."

THE MARRIAGE OF THE LAMB

Jesus the Chatan (Bridegroom) walked to a table upon which was a Cup of wine.
He took it, lifted it up to His mouth and drank it.

Then every Saint who is a part of the Kalah (Bride) took their cup of wine.
Each raised it up and drank it.

The Wedding Ceremony was concluded.

It was time for the Bridegroom and Bride to enter the New Jerusalem.
Jesus pointed to the East and we turned around to see what He was pointing at.
The sky opened.
There before our eyes was a huge city.
It towered high beaming out rainbow streams of light.

Around it was a red-yellow light the color of jasper.
The city was pure gold, like clear glass.
It had twelve gates that were made of pearl:
The streets leading to it and within were of pure gold, like transparent glass.
Then Jesus said -

"I promised to prepare a place for you.
It has met the approval of God My Father.
I have finished it and now you can live with Me forever in the New Jerusalem.
This is the place I specially prepared for you.
John 14:2-3
It is time for us to enter.
Let us enter and enjoy its Glory."

Then He pointed to it.
(In all Jewish weddings, the bridegroom and bride enter a Huppah where the nuptials take place.
This was our Heavenly Huppah, where we would be united with Jesus Christ forever.)

As far as the eye could see, countless millions of Saints in pure white garments prepared to enter.
They participated in the recessional and walked in the direction of the New Jerusalem.
Each group proceeded to the Gate assigned for them to enter.
There were mighty Angels at each gate to welcome and usher us in.

Separately the entourage of 144,000 Virgins led Jesus through the Eastern Gate.

In a moment we were supernaturally translated into the New Jerusalem.
Each of us found ourselves in our own Mansion.

And so it was that we took up our residence in the Holy City of the Lamb. Revelation 21:9-23

Chapter Eight

The Millennial reign of Jesus Christ and His Bride

Our return to earth

THE APOCALYPSE THEN GLORY

A message came that it was time for Jesus Christ to return to the Earth.
We had already taken up residence in the New Jerusalem when the announcement came.
At this time we were supernaturally transported out of the City.
Each of us was carefully placed on a beautiful white Horse.
There were countless millions of Saints on horses.
We were ready to embark on this exciting journey.
We found ourselves in perfect rank as pre-determined by Jesus.
I couldn't wait to participate in one of the greatest events of all time and eternity.

In front of us were an innumerable company of Angels led by Gabriel the Archangel.
In front of them seven Trumpeters took their place.
One of them was preparing to sound the great Trumpet Sound.
The Second Coming of Jesus Christ to the Earth was about to commence.
It was time to descend to the Earth.

Then Jesus appeared riding a magnificent White Horse.
A white cloud formed around Him and raised Him up into the air.
We looked at Him in wonder and admiration.

Michael the Archangel made a loud announcement -
"Behold, He that rides is Faithful and True.
In righteousness he judges and makes war.
He is the Word of God."

THE MILLENNIAL REIGN OF JESUS CHRIST AND HIS BRIDE

As we looked at Jesus, His eyes were as a flame of fire.
On his head were many crowns.
He had a name written on Him that none of us knew.
He was clothed with vesture dipped in blood.
Out of His mouth went a sharp Sword.
On his thigh a Name was written -
KING OF KINGS, AND LORD OF LORDS.
Then the trumpeter sounded and it was the signal for the descent to begin.
The sound echoed throughout Heaven and descended to the Earth

An angel came out of the temple, crying with a loud voice to Jesus -
"Thrust in thy sickle, and reap:
The time is come for thee to reap; for the harvest of the earth is ripe.
The winepress will be trodden without the city.
Blood will come out of the winepress, even unto the horse bridles.
It will be by the space of a thousand, six hundred furlongs." Revelation 14:15, 20

I remembered that Enoch had prophesied about this event, saying -
"Behold, the Lord cometh with ten thousands of his Saints." Jude 14

The Second Coming of Christ was unfolding before our eyes.
We were seeing it from a Heavenly perspective.
The descent was with great power.

It was as if Heaven was coming to Earth.
We passed through a blackened Universe that had been greatly shaken.
The Earth was in darkness with sulfurous fires burning everywhere.
It had tilted on its axis and destruction was everywhere.
It was experiencing its final hours.

Suddenly Jesus spoke with a Powerful Voice.
The Atmosphere parted before Him and the sky was rent open.
He appeared several miles above Israel and the Valley of Armageddon.
The sky was filled with Angels and the Army of the Saints on white horses, behind Him.

Below, the valley was filled with millions of soldiers of the Antichrist.
They were approaching Jerusalem to destroy it.
Suddenly Jesus shouted with a thunderous voice - "Enough.
I bring judgment to Lucifer, the Antichrist, the False Prophet and their followers."

A sharp sword went out of His mouth.
Within mille-seconds it cut, lacerated and destroyed every soldier and horse before Him.
The Valley of Armageddon was filled with rivers of blood and dead corpses lay everywhere.
Revelation 16:16

Then Michael the Archangel descended with great strength and Lucifer was struck to the ground.
Within seconds Lucifer was bound with chains.

The Earth opened up and he was cast down into the bottomless pit.

Other Angels captured and bound the Antichrist and False Prophet.
For them there was no place to hide.
They were cast through the opened Earth into the flaming fires of Sheol.
Their screams echoed as they fell into the burning flames.

Then Jesus spoke to the Angels and said -
"Go to the ends of the Earth.
Separate the Evil Nations from the Good Nations.
Those who have afflicted My people Israel are evil.
Cast them into the lake of fire.
Those who have been good to Israel may live on the Earth under My Rule."

Great light shone from Jesus and it lit the whole earth.
Immediately darkness dissipated and disappeared.
Then Jesus spoke these creative words and said –
"Let the earth be restored as in the days of the Garden of Eden.
Let the Mountains, valleys, seas and rivers be renewed.
Let the Earth be filled with lush vegetation, animals and all living creatures.
Let birds fly in the sky and let there be fish in the streams, rivers and oceans.
Let the Nations and People that are on the Earth be healed and restored.
Let there be Peace on Earth and Goodwill to all people and creation."

The creative Power of the Messiah was plain for all to see.
There was a hush everywhere and a peaceful atmosphere filled the air.
Before our eyes the world suddenly changed and became beautiful.

There was a cheer that came throughout the ranks of the Armies of the Saints.
It echoed throughout the earth.
"Great is the Lord and greatly to be praised."
The Angels sang -
"Peace on Earth and goodwill to all men.
For unto thee a King is given.
His Name is Wonderful, Counselor, the Mighty God, the Everlasting Father, and the Prince of Peace."

Then a resounding voice came from God the Father in Heaven that said -
"This is My beloved Son in whom I am well pleased. I decree Him to be King of Kings and Lord of Lords over all the Earth."

The gathering together of Israel
Jesus then commanded the Angels to gather all the Children of Israel from the four corners of the Earth.
It included those who had escaped to Petra where they were in hiding in underground caves.
They had fled there, to escape the wrath of satan and the antichrist.
The Angels brought all of Israel back to Jerusalem to assemble at the Mount of Olives.
Several million Israelites covered the whole area.
Then they looked up and saw Jesus on a cloud descending on to the Mt of Olives.

As His feet touched the mountain, there was a thunderous sound and it split down the middle.

He came down to where the people were and walked amongst them.
He stretched out His hands to them.
They could see the nail scarred wounds He had received at His crucifixion.
They fell on their faces before Him wailing and crying.
"Yeshua Ha'Mashiach" they cried.
"Yeshua Ha'Mashiach" they said, over and over again.

Then Jesus spoke with a loud voice and everyone heard Him say -
"I am your Messiah and I have come to rescue you and set up My Kingdom upon the Earth.
You are my people and from this moment I will reign over you and take care of you."

Another prophecy had been fulfilled -
"Behold, He cometh with clouds; and every eye shall see him, and they also which pierced him: and all people of the earth shall wail because of him."
Revelation 1:7
Then as I looked toward the east, I saw the New Jerusalem descending through the atmosphere toward us.
It came above us and hung in the air.
It was gigantic and magnificent.
Instantaneously all the Saints were translated from their white horsed into it.
Once again I found myself in my beautiful Mansion.

Chapter Nine

The New Jerusalem

Location
Often in our Bible Studies on earth, we spoke about the Millennial New Jerusalem.
Here are some of the calculations we had made, that come to mind.
The city is a cube of 12,000 furlongs.
One furlong is 600 feet and that makes the city 1363 miles long, wide and high.

If each floor was I mile high, there would be 1363 floors.
Each floor would then have about 2 million square miles of space.
If only 20% was used for dwellings, 20 billion people could be accommodated comfortably.
Each person would have about 10 acres of space.
By comparison:
New York is 1,458 square miles
and has a population of 19 million people.
London is 659 square miles
and has a population of 14 million people.

I now was actually living in the New Jerusalem.
Those calculations we made, did not come close to the reality.

The city itself is made of pure gold like clear glass.
It reaches high into Heavens and can be seen glistening in its glorious light, hundreds of miles away.
It is located high above Jerusalem, which is the world capital.
It is the City described in Revelation 21:19-20.

The New Jerusalem is built on a gigantic and brilliant foundation made up of 12 layers which are –
Jasper,
Sapphire,
Chalcedony,
Emerald,
Sardonyx,
Sardius,
Chrysolite,
Beryl,

THE NEW JERUSALEM

Topaz,
Chrysoprase,
Jacinth,
and Amethyst.

Jesus mentioned that He had created this foundational structure of the City for two reasons -
- One was for beauty
- The other for structural strength.
The structural strength of each precious stone, at each different level was strategically designed.
Combined it is strong enough to carry a city that is 1363 miles high.
Jesus inscribed the names of the 12 Apostles in the foundation.
This was because they are the foundation of the Church.

It is surrounded by a wall 200 feet high made of opaque jasper.
This is red, yellow and brown quartz, with a smooth highly polished surface.
In the wall around the city are 12 gates and each is made of pearl.
Inscribed on each gate is the name of one of the Tribes of Israel.
At each gate is a magnificent Angel standing guard and entry is by special invitation only.
Only those who are written in the Book of Life are allowed to come in and out. Rev 21:12-13, 27

The Eastern gate is a very special Gate.
In Old Testament times, the glory of the LORD always came through this gate.
It came from the east and filled the Temple.

It is the gate reserved only for Jesus Christ, the King of Kings.
It is the gate through which He made His glorious entry after His Second Coming.
It is kept shut and only used for His convenience.
Ezekiel 43:2-7, Ezekiel 44:2-3
Another interesting aspect is that the New Jerusalem is connected to Heaven.
I never understood the symbolical significance of the dream that Jacob had.
His dream was of a ladder ascending from Bethel or the house of God into Heaven.
This dream is symbolical of the New Jerusalem that is connected to Heaven.
There is much of this that is far beyond imagination or description.
This way to Heaven is open and at any time God may reveal His Face to His Children.
For the rest of eternity we will have a direct relationship with Him.
We will continue to grow in our knowledge of God and experience His blessings and goodness.
We also have His Name on our foreheads.
Revelation 21:4

A pure River of Life flows from under Jesus Throne.
Revelation 22:1-2
It continues through the city in the middle of the golden Highway.
On each side of the River and the middle are Trees of life.
They bare twelve fruits, one each month and these fruits are preserved for Overcomer's.
The leaves of the tree are used to bring healing to people of the earth that are sick.

God's Presence, Glory and Light is manifest throughout the City and from there throughout the earth.
There is no darkness or night on the earth.

When I was on earth I experienced five dimensions – time, space, matter, motion and light.
Scientists had also discovered other dimensions relating to the universe.
After arriving in Heaven I discovered that they were transcended by many other dimensions.

In Heaven we experienced timelessness and continue to do so in the New Jerusalem.
Whenever desired, we may travel at the speed of thought anywhere within our allowed estate.
By that I mean that the thought of being somewhere, places us there.
However I love taking walks within the City.
It allows me to discover and enjoy its distinctive design and beauty.
There are no elevators.

An architectural wonder.
Wide streets of Gold lead from the twelve Gates into the City.
Branching off from them are smaller streets.
Each floor is very similar.
When going to my Home I would enter a 1000 feet high Atrium.
Its walls and floors are made of rich, highly polished marble in pastel colors.
The marble is skillfully cut and the colors perfectly matched.
It creates a soft affluence.

The balustrades leading up from it are crafted in
polished brass and have a warm effect.
They lead up to an area that is unique and royal.
Its creativety is brilliant.
It is said that all the architects that have ever lived,
together could not have designed anything like it.

The corridors leading from there are spacious.
They have arts and crafts that have been tastefully
placed along the way.
There are statues that rise up to thirty feet and each
is significant.
They symbolize attributes of compassion, strength,
humility, prayer and others.
One is of Samson killing the lion.
Another is of Jacob wresting with the Angel.
Other crafts are small and intricate, designed to
catch the attention and awe of those passing by.
Each is spiritually significant.
These corridors lead to all kinds and sizes of
Rooms.

The drapes and curtains in these Rooms are
tastefully hung to enhance the design.
They are made of exquisite kinds of cloth and
different textures.
Some are made of silk and are sleek and smooth.
Others are woven of a thicker kind of thread, are
heavier and have a warmer effect.

Hand crafted and finely embroidered cloths cover
tables.
They have vases, pottery and china neatly placed on
them.

THE NEW JERUSALEM

Truly the New Jerusalem is an exciting place.
There are many wonderful places to discover and experiences to enjoy.
There is constant renewal.
It would take an eternity to explore these wonders.

Before taking you into my Home, let me take you to other parts of the City first.
In whatever direction you go, the golden streets will lead you to amazing places.

The Conference Centers are where Teaching is given and Ministry assignments are prepared.
These are places where Saints talk, share ideas and prepare.
It never occurred to me that throughout eternity, the Saints would continue to enjoy teaching and ministry.

There are large Auditoriums where the Choirs and Singers rehearse for events.
Often I sit and listen to them.

There are large places where Festivities, Passovers and Commemorations are held.

We always enjoy coming together for Corporate Prayer.
There are special locations for this.
The larger ones are very similar to amphitheaters.
The smaller ones however are quite different.
There is a smaller one that is a replica of the Upper Room of Pentecost.
These times of prayer are always led by Prayer Leaders.

Here special manifestations of Gods Glory occur and are wonderful and refreshing.

One of the prayers we prayed in unison is -
"Our Father in Heaven, Your Name is Holy.
May Your Kingdom come and will be done here and on Earth as in Heaven.
Thank you for all of Your love, provisions, gifts and an eternal home.
Thank you for salvation, delivering us from evil and cleansing us with the precious Blood of Jesus.
Father, the Kingdom, Power and Glory belong to You alone forever.
Amen,

There is a huge Paradise Garden in the middle of the City on each floor.
It has the unique aspect of having many Children Centers around it.
Here Caregivers spend much time caring for and playing with the Children.

As one browses through the streets, there are many special places of interest.
These are places where Designing, Pottery, Weaving and Embroidery are done.
Garments are made for the Feasts and Special Occasions.
The making of precious Jewelry and Crowns are done at other locations.

The New Jerusalem is a magnificent City.
When taking other excursions you will find special places where artists do their paintings.

THE NEW JERUSALEM

Its enjoyable to take leisurely walks through these areas.
I especially like walking through the beautiful gardens.

Two wonderful places to visit are -
The Memorial Center.
Here the sacrifices, bravery and achievements of Saints are commemorated.
This covers the 6000 year history of the old earth.
The details were recorded and prepared by Angels.
They are accurate and specific.

The Library.
Here one finds enlightening, edifying, helpful books of any description.
Among others:
A Book of the Living with the names of all who are Children of the Most High God.
A Book with the Historical Record of all time.
A Book on the Eternal Purposes of God.
A Book covering all aspects of the New Jerusalem.
A Book, similar to Genesis, describing the restoration of the Apocalypse Earth.
A Book on all the Laws of the New Earth, promulgated by Jesus Christ, King of Kings.
There are all kinds of informational and educational Books one could ever desire to read.

Leading away from the many Atriums throughout the City are **Banquet rooms.**
They are for formal and informal gatherings, receptions and festivities.
They feature Commemorations, Celebrations and Re-unions.

They are for larger or smaller groups.

First there are many **Commemorations** held.
Each one has its own unique characteristics and function.

There is the Commemoration of the Godhead
God the Father, Jesus Christ His Son and the Holy Spirit are acknowledged for who they are.
The intrinsic value of their attributes is highlighted.
The greater depths of their love, mercy, grace, power, wisdom, knowledge and truth is revealed.
It is wonderful to receive greater revelation and understanding of them.
Truly the Apostle Paul wrote – "We would know even as we are known."

Another is the Commemoration of the Passover
The Saints gather together to remember the millions of Lambs sacrificed for the sins of Israel.
We thank God for the deliverance of Israel from Egypt.
We remember the supreme sacrifice of the Jesus Christ the Lamb of God.
We express our thanks to God for delivering us from satan and his kingdom of darkness.
This event is very much like the Passover that was kept by the Israelites.

Then there is the Commemoration of Gods Gifts of Grace
We remember the gifts of salvation, healing, deliverance, restoration, provision and blessing.
These are the wonderful gifts we experienced on Earth and the World continues to do so.

We continue to participate in these blessings by the gathering of the healing leaves and Priestly Ministry.
At this Commemoration we continue to receive testimonies of people on Earth being blessed.
There are many of healings and miracles that are taking place.
There are also reports of the teaching and preaching of Kingdom of God to the people all over the world.

Second there are various kinds of **celebrations.**
They are always coupled with feasting and dancing.

Let me mention some of the Celebrations –
The Celebration of Ministering Angels.
This is one of the most interesting events held from time to time.
All are invited to attend and it is immensely enjoyed by everyone.
Saints are invited to share their Angelic experiences and encounters.
Those Angels who helped us on Earth are there to be thanked and honored.
It is amazing to see them and hear their recollections.

There were two that were most impressive to me.
The one was the Angel who stopped the mouths of the Lions in Daniels lion's den.
The other was the Angel who strengthened Jesus in the Garden of Gethsemane.
There are many others and during eternity we will enjoy celebrating them.
Their service, faithfulness and beauty is greatly appreciated.

The Celebration of Victories.
During these events we celebrate past spiritual battles and victories.
The Saints reflect on the Spiritual Battles they fought.
They give testimonies of the victories they experienced.
There are so many wonderful, interesting and inspiring stories to hear.
I am glad that we have eternity to listen to all of them.
This is one event that I greatly look forward to attending over and over again.

The Celebration of Service.
Every Saint does Service in the New Jerusalem.
It is a place of activity and motion.
The Lord has given each of us our assignments and they are perfectly suited for us.
Everything we do is easy and can be performed successfully.
On these special occasions Saints come together to show the unique service they render.
Everyone receives recognition for what they do.
It is so interesting to interact with so many gifted and talented Saints.

The Celebration of inheritance.
There is no end to the riches that Jesus obtained from God the Father.
It by far transcends the Earthly idea of wealth.
It is far beyond gold, silver, jewels, property and real estate.
It is so vast that only eternal time can reveal it.

The Saints are blessed to have become joint heirs with Christ.
What they have inherited is continuously being revealed and celebrated.

The Celebration of Abundance.
These are special occasions when the King surprises the Saints.
They are always different and exciting.
The saints are invited to attend and feast on the best foods, delicacies and wines from His Table.
There are always wonderful gifts for everyone.
The Kingdom of our Lord Jesus Christ is luxurious and prosperous.

Third there are many **Reunions** –
On these occasions' close and distant family members spend precious time together.
At times close friends are also invited.
These are very similar to Earthly Reunions, but have a Heavenly accent.

Now let me walk you through my magnificent home located on the Northern side.
It has the most wonderful atmosphere.
Wherever you are in it you hear soothing music playing in the background.
It is celestial, satisfying and flows like a gentle breeze.

Everything one could ever dream of is provided.
There is an abundance of delicious food and drinks of which most are new to me.
The water is pure and refreshing.

THE APOCALYPSE THEN GLORY

My large walk in closet has all kinds of clothes, robes and garments, for all different occasions.
The Royal clothing combinations are separate from the others.

During my earthly Ministry I remember speaking to a Hindu Convert.
He experienced being translated into Heaven after his conversion.
Jesus showed him Heaven and his Heavenly Mansion.
While sharing his testimony with us, he described it to us.
Certainly what he tried to describe did not come close to what I was experiencing.

The furnishings were perfect, beautiful and comfortable.
A large 30 seat wood table and chairs were intricately carved beyond description.
The table settings were perfectly matched and color coordinated. There were many luxurious, comfortable couches and chairs.
Here and there in the house, decorative vases, pottery and moldings were strategically placed.
It accentuated different features of the house.
Living there, made me feel special and royal.
I loved walking out of my home into a beautiful garden that was always self contained.
The greenery, trees, flowers were colorful and its fruitfulness and beauty beyond description.
I treated each plant, tree and blade of grass with tender loving care.

When Family and Friends came to visit, everything was available for wonderful fellowship.
It by far exceeded anything I had known when I lived in the old world.
We enjoyed eating together and talking around the table.
We sat on leisurely chairs or in the garden having fellowship.
At times we made music and sang together.
We always began and ended these times with prayer and thanksgiving to God.

At all times I enjoyed the most satisfying peace, security and rest.
I knew I was forever loved and protected by the Creator and Ruler of all things.
How true are the words of the scripture -
"Thou shalt also be a crown of glory in the hand of the LORD, and a royal diadem in the hand of thy God.
And they shall call them, the holy people, the redeemed of the LORD: and thou shalt be called, Sought out, A city not forsaken."
Isaiah 62:1-4, 11, 12
"And thus shall we always be with the Lord."
I Thessalonians 4:17

Chapter Ten

The City of Jerusalem on Earth

Beneath the New Jerusalem is the earthly city of Jerusalem.
They are distinctly separated.

Jerusalem is destined to continue, world without end.
It is at the center of the renewed land of Israel and the World.

There is a *sacred area*, eight miles long and six miles wide at its center.
At its center is the Temple and it is completely surrounded by an open space, eighty-four feet wide.

In the Sacred Area are the houses of the Priests and the Levites.

Each has a section, eight miles long and three miles wide

Jerusalem lies next to the Sacred Area and is the Capital City of Israel.
There is another area on its eastern and western side that stretches across the whole land.
It is reserved only for Jesus Christ, King of Kings.
Ezekiel 45:1-8

The twelve tribes of Israel also have their land allotments.
From the northern border of Syria to the southern border of Egypt the tribes have been placed in this order:
Dan
Asher
Naphtali
Manasseh
Ephraim
Reuben
Judah
Benjamin
Simeon
Issachar
Zebulon
Gad
Ezekiel 48:1-35

To the children of Israel God made a promise and it has been fulfilled.
Their waste cities have been rebuilt and inhabited.
Their Vineyards and Gardens are fruitful and will never be pulled up again. Amos 9:14

Mountains sides are producing new wine and the hills are flowing with milk.
The rivers of Judah are flowing and the waters from the house of the LORD are gushing into the valley. Joel 3:18
The Israelites are dancing under their grape vines in abundance. Jeremiah 31:5
Israel will never be ashamed again. Joel 2:26

I mentioned that at the heart of the City is the Temple built by Jesus Christ.
It has a new Altar. Zechariah 6:12
Burnt sacrifices and offerings are made upon it every day for Israel and the World. Isaiah 56:7
The Temple has a new Priesthood. Revelation 20:6
Special times of fasting is directed by them for all peoples. Zechariah 8:4
The Temple is designated as God's house of prayer for all nations. Ezekiel 40:38-43
Praises to God ascend from it constantly. Isaiah12:12
From there the Sabbath and other Feast Days are directed and observed by the Israelites.

The whole Earth has been remade.
The Earth has been restored on its axis.
What was broken has been fixed.
The continents, lands and waterways are restored.
Everything that is sinful, hurtful, harmful, intimidating and embarrassing has been removed.
Nature and all forms of life are renewed like the time of the Garden of Eden.
All forms of life live together in harmony.
The wolf and the lamb feed together. Isaiah 65:17-23.

Life expectancy has changed and people live hundreds of years. Isaiah 60:5

Life on Earth has radically changed and goes on.

Setting up the New Millennial World Government

Mighty Angels appeared to the Nations throughout the World.
Their important announcement included the following statement -

- Jesus Christ has declared Himself to be King of Kings and Lord of Lords over all the Earth.
- His Government is an Absolute Monarchy.
- As Supreme Monarch He alone has all the power.
- He makes, ratifies or rescinds laws that are binding upon all the Nations and people of Earth.
- He has selected and appointed Kings over all the Nations.
- These Kings would be His emissaries to appoint a Government for each nation.
- That the New World would be a wonderful place creating:

Peace
Prosperity
Abundance
Health
Knowledge
Care for all
Employment for all
Security
Justice for all

Kingship
Saints were selected by Jesus for Kingship.
They were summoned to appear before Him in His Throne Room in the New Jerusalem.
It was surprising to see many humble an unknown Saints receiving this pinnacle reward.

Again a promise was fulfilled that Jesus had made -
Revelation 20:4
And I saw thrones, and they sat upon them, and judgment was given unto them: They lived and reigned with Christ a thousand years.
Revelation 2:26-27
He that overcometh, and keepeth my works unto the end, to him will I give power over the nations: And he shall rule them with a rod of iron.
Revelation 1:6
And hath made us Kings unto God and his Father.
Luke 19:17
Well done, thou good servant: because thou hast been faithful in a very little, have thou authority over ten cities.

These selected Saints were summoned by Michael the Archangel and brought to the Throne Room.
There Jesus gave them their assignment and what they were required to do and say.
They were also given a special Message to be read to the Government and Nation they were visiting.
They were dressed as Kings with magnificent clothes, robes, jewels, a gold crown and a royal scepter.
On the crown was inscribed the words -
"In service of Jesus Christ, King of Kings."

These Royal designated Sovereigns made their journey to their selected Nation of the World.

On one occasion we were enjoying conversation and one of the Saints with whom we were fellowshipping was Mark.
He was one of the Royal Designates that had been sent on Kingly Business.
He was sent to a country previously known as England.
He shared this experience with us.

His transportation was supernatural and took milleseconds from the New Jerusalem to England.
Waiting for him at the entrance of their New Parliament Building was Ruben Eberstein.
He had been appointed by Jesus as World Government Coordinator and special Emissary.

The Government of Jesus Christ is not a Democracy.
It is a Theocracy.
The whole world is governed under Him.

This was prophesied by Isaiah -
"The Government shall be upon His shoulder." Isaiah 9:6-7.

In England, Mark received a royal welcome and was ushered into a magnificent new Building.
In the Banquet Room they all enjoyed a wonderful festive Dinner.
Different speakers spoke -
One gave a report of the progress and achievements that had been made to re-develop England.

Another speaker brought to remembrance the rich spiritual history of England.
It was mentioned that England had sent many Bibles and Missionaries throughout the old world.
The aspiring President of England spoke of the dreams and aspirations he had for his Nation.
The World President gave special thanks and honor to Jesus Christ the King, for all He had done.
He was praised for saving and recreating the World and giving it a glorious future.

Then Mark was asked to receive special gifts for Jesus.
He thanked them for the special way he was received and the protocol they followed.
He assured them that it brought great honor to Jesus Christ the King of Kings.

The President of England who had been appointed by Divine decree was inducted.
The twelve Cabinet Members he had selected were introduced and appointed.
They would advise Him on matters within each of their Departments.
The Government was declared to be set in motion.

The twelve Cabinet positions and Departments are the same in all Countries and are -
Agriculture
Finance
Education
Energy
Health
Compassionate Services
Housing and Farming

Interior
Labor
Law
State
Transportation

There is no War department because it is not needed.
Isaiah had made this prophetic promise -
"They shall beat their swords into plowshares, and neither shall they learn war anymore." Isaiah 2:4

Each State and City has its own local Government.
It has an appointed Governor or Mayor and twelve Department Heads.
It is similar to the National Cabinet.
Each answers to their own particular State or higher Cabinet Member.

I asked Mark about what was going on in the newly restored world.
I was interested to know how people were living in the Millennial Kingdom.
Mark continued to share more information with us.

The World has only one legal and justice system
It is based on the Ten Commandments.
From Jerusalem, teachers are sent to teach the ways of the Lord.
The Earth is being filled with the Knowledge of the Lord.

All Ordinances are written and published.

THE CITY OF JERUSALEM ON EARTH

They are required to be kept and the punishment of breaking the law has severe consequences.

As a result of this new form of Government -
- All forms of oppression are banished and there is justice for all.
- Righteousness has sprung up among the Nations.
- The needy are helped.

Israel is flourishing economically, agriculturally and scientifically.
She has been greatly blessed and has an abundance of everything.
Israel has become a great source of supply to all the Nations.
The knowledge and wisdom she has acquired, is generously shared with all.
In order to enjoy this blessing preconditions have been set.
Jesus requires the following:

Every person on Earth must keep the Feast of Tabernacles in October each year.

At this time the Leaders of the Nations are required to bring gifts to honor Jesus the King of Kings.
In this way they show obeisance and their subjection to Him.
Those who refuse are punished and the Nation that refuses to submit to the laws of Jesus suffers famine. (Isaiah 60:5)

Jesus Christ the Son of God is the personification of Kingly perfection.

His Reign, Laws and Government, have come like a fresh breath of air to the world.
The world has been rescued from chaos, has been transformed and is prosperous.
His rule is exactly what the world was waiting for.

Economically the world now knows no depression or inflation.
The World Treasury is secure.
It has one financial system and one budget and God guarantees everything.
He is the ultimate source and supply.
There are no Secret Societies, Organizations or the Mafia to manipulate the outcome of anything.
Political Parties don't exist.

The World Economy is easy for all to understand.
Factories are created to meet the needs of consumers.
Farms plant and grow whatever agricultural needs of communities are.
Livestock farmers raise enough animals to satisfy requirements.
Every person receives fair wages.
People are subject to their local, state and national Government, who provide for them.
National Governments are Subject to the Kingship provided by Jesus Christ, King of Kings.
Millionaires and financial Tycoons do not exist in this New World.
There is no power grabbing.
Everything is done with transparency and openness.

The Educational Institutions are sound, fair and balanced.
The purpose of all education is to provide the best information and science.
It is to build character in people's lives.
It serves to enhance culture in society.
It is wholesome and all questions are answered.
It ultimately enables people to follow their career dreams and experience job satisfaction.
It provides amazing scientific and technological breakthroughs improving all spheres of life.

The provision of energy in the world is significantly different.
It no longer is nuclear or oil based.
It operates on technology far more advanced than that of fusion.
It does not contaminate and meets every energy need in the world.

The world has become a healthy and beautiful place to live in.
Nutrition is of great importance in the New World and everything needed is available.
Most people eat vegetables, fruits, berries, nuts and dairy products in their diet.
They work, exercise and live in a clean environment.
They are stress free and healthy.

Sickness and disease is seldom heard of.
When it manifests it is promptly and aggressively dealt with.
Sickness and disease are treated in four ways -

First
By Prevention.

Second
Herbal treatment from leaves of the Tree of Life growing in Jerusalem.
This was foretold in Revelation 22:1-4
"He showed me a pure river of water of life, clear as crystal, proceeding out of the throne of God and of the Lamb. In the midst of the street of it, and on either side of the river, was there the tree of life, and the leaves of the tree were for the healing of the nations."

Third
Supernatural miracles and healings that are done by Angels.
An example of this was the moving of the water at the Pool of Bethesda in the time of Christ.
People are told where Angels manifest their presence and patiently wait for the time to receive a miracle.

Fourth
Special supernatural healings and miracles are performed by the Priests in Jerusalem.
Special sacrifices are made and procedures followed by those in need and receive answers to prayer.
This Ministry focuses on Gods power and goodness.

Compassionate Services ensure that the needy are taken care of.
There is no homelessness due to unemployment, addictions or emotional and mental problems.

These kinds of problems are immediately addressed with compassion.
Widows, Orphans and the Elderly are showered with compassion and care.
The Government generously provides every needed facility and program to help them.
There is no worry or concern about any contingency or retirement.

The world truly has become a place of opportunity, productivity, prosperity and success.
It is a place where needs are met and life is enjoyed.

City planning
The first responsibility of any of the Governments is the planning and rebuilding of New Cities.
Specific guidelines have been laid down by Jesus Christ Himself and are strictly adhered to.
The cities have -
Factories for manufacturing.
Office buildings for business.
Facilities for different kinds of Service.
Education campuses.
Medical and Health Centers.
Markets for all kinds of foods and products.
Parks.
Recreation and Sport facilities
Resorts for relaxation and leisure.

The Cities ensure an atmosphere of -
True Godliness
Temples have been built to provide and advance the Teachings of Jesus Christ.
No other religion or teaching is allowed on the earth.

People worship and serve Jehovah God, Jesus Christ and the Holy Spirit.

Righteousness
People are taught and encouraged to do the right things in life, wherever they are.

Cleanliness
Strict health laws have been implemented.
Each city has wonderful pure water, energy and utility systems.
The ablution, disease control and healthcare facilities are of the highest standard.

Excellence
Buildings, streets, parks and recreation centers are built to a very high standard of excellence.
They reflect quality, efficiency and beauty.
The beauty of the parks and gardens around the city and homes are breathtaking.

Abundance
An estimated one billion people on Earth are provided with spacious cities, farms and homes.
The land is fruitful, the rains frequent and the produce abundant.

Houses are built to completely satisfy the needs of people.
Every husband, wife and family is provided a beautiful home.
Houses of different sizes are built to accommodate smaller and larger families.
Furniture, home appliances and household necessities are provided.

Different kinds of vehicles are available to meet every need.

Farms are located throughout the rural areas.
Those wanting to farm are given special training to be effective farmers.
They are provided with farmland and state of the art farming equipment.
They continually receive ongoing updated education and training.
True organic seed, plants and trees are provided to produce the best crops.
There are no genetically engineered seeds or plants.
Quality animals are provided to farmers to breed their herds and stock.
Farmers do not have to contend with briers and weeds when farming.
There is no inclement weather, droughts or storms.
Harvests and food production remain highly effective.
It is easy and lucrative to successfully market products.
There is no manipulation of the market and fluctuating prices.

Jobs
Work opportunities are always readily available.
Everyone is provided a job within their profile and ability.
Production expectations are within reason, without unrealistic expectations.
Hard work and productivity is graciously awarded.
Reasonable working hours have been implemented.
There is Monday through Friday, eight hours per day work schedules.

Workers spend weekends with their families.
An annual one month vacation is given to each worker.
Fairness in the workplace and the promotion of good workers is paramount.

Factories
Factories are planned and built to be safe and eco friendly.
Nature and the environment is always highly protected and preserved.
Energy is not fossil fuel based.
There is no smoke, chemical or other contamination.
Canning factories preserve vegetables, fruit and meat products, using new technologies that are healthy.
No preservatives or artificial flavorings are added.
New technologies are constantly developed to provide efficiency and productivity.

There is no doubt that the New World is a much better place to live in when compared to the old one that was under satans control.

Chapter Eleven

The Wedding Feast

The Wedding of Jesus Christ to His Bride was the greatest wedding reception of all time.
It could only be described as Regal, Perfect and Grandiose.

This Wedding Feast was in the New Jerusalem.
It followed after the Marriage that had taken place in Heaven.

God the Father decreed that it would take place on Earth so that the Israelites could attend.
Matthew 22:2
"The kingdom of heaven is like unto a certain king, which made a marriage for his son."
Isaiah 25:6
"And in this mountain shall the LORD of hosts make unto all people a feast of fat things, a feast of wines on the lees, of fat things full of marrow, of wines on the lees well refined."

And so God provided this amazing Feast.
- The venue was perfect and luxurious.
- The spread of food and drinks was bountiful, beyond description.
- The program was most enjoyable.
- The experience was unforgettable.

The arrival of international Guests
On the southern side of the Temple Mount is the Royal Palace.
There the twelve Apostles sit on Thrones, judging Israel.
Next to it are accommodations for special guests visiting Jerusalem.

The international guests arrived one by one.
Together with their entourage they were escorted to the comfortable residence provided for them.

The Master of the Palace Household always takes care of the hospitality, catering and housekeeping arrangements at this royal residence.
He ensures that all the State Rooms and guest rooms are in perfect condition.
In Jerusalem, Guests are privileged to see a Government operating in perfection and excellence.
The likes of this have never been seen before in human history.

The Venue for the Marriage Feast was the Festive Chamber in the New Jerusalem.
It was specifically made for the great Wedding Feast of Jesus Christ.
It is situated on a lower level and large enough to accommodate millions of guests.

The main Eastern part was reserved for the
Bridegroom and His Bride the Saints.
The tables were set in such a way that every Saint
could see the Bridegroom in the middle.
He was the focal Person of attention.
In front of His Table was a Gold Table and on it a
White Book.
In it is written the names of all the Saints who were
a part of His Bride.

The Festive Chamber had twelve entrances from the
outside.
The floor gently slopes downward towards the front,
enabling everyone to see all the activities.
The tables were spaciously placed providing a very
friendly atmosphere.
Millions of Jews from the twelve different tribes were
ushered in to take their place.

Then the Leaders from different Nations of the earth
were brought in.
Only those who qualified were permitted entrance.
The dress code was formal.
They brought special wedding gifts for Jesus Christ.
These were received, notated and placed on special
gift tables provided for that purpose.
To enter this Chamber was an unforgettable
experience..
Leaders would share this experience with their
Nation when they got home.

Arrival of the Special Guests
These special guests came by Royal Invitation.
"Blessed are they which are called unto the
marriage supper of the Lamb." Revelation 19:5

They were Old Testament Saints that had been resurrected with Christ and taken to Heaven.
Among them was one of the greatest Prophets, John the Baptist.
He described himself as a friend of the Bridegroom. John 3:29

It was amazing to see these millions of Guests making their appearance.
They came directly from Heaven and entered through huge doors into the Wedding Chamber.
They walked to the reserved area and tables prepared for them.
They were led by the great Patriarch Abraham.
They came elegantly dressed and stately.
Among them were Adam, Eve, Noah, Isaac, Jacob, Joshua, Job, Samuel, David, Solomon, Esther, and Daniel.
The International and Jewish guests were whispering to each other as they recognized many of them.

Arrival of the Bride
King David had prophesied -
With gladness and rejoicing the Bride of the Messiah shall be brought in and enter into the Palace of the Great King. Psalm 45:7-15

Our way of entrance was through stairways coming from the upper levels.
We did not enter until all the guests had taken their place.
At this time the ushering Angels directed us to enter through the seven upper entrances.
We came down stairs from the northern side of the Chamber.

Our entrance was timely, perfect and gracious.
We sat down at the tables specially reserved for us.
Now we were waiting for the arrival of our Heavenly Bridegroom.

Spectacular arrival of Jesus Christ
On the Eastern side, two main doors at the center of the Bridal Chamber opened.
Seven trumpeters stood there with golden trumpets.
There was a hush all over as everyone waited with great expectation.
The moment had arrived for the Bridegroom to make His appearance.
We were greeted with a regal fanfare, played on long herald trumpets.
Each trumpet had a long elegant banner hanging from it.
The echoing sound brought a thrill and excitement as they played -
"Oh come righteous King of Grace."

From either side of them 144,000 Jewish virgins of the twelve tribes of Israel came dancing.
They took their place on a lower setting at tables in front of the trumpeters.

Again the trumpeters heralded as they played -
"Let us rejoice and be glad, for the Bridegroom has come."

And there He stood as the central point of attraction.
He was clothed with a white shining linen garment down to His feet.
Around His chest he had a golden girdle.

His hair was like pure white wool hanging down to His shoulders.
Upon it was a dazzling crown of gold with large priceless gems.
His eyes were as a flame of fire.
His countenance shone.
His feet were like refined brass.
He went and took the White Book that was on the Golden Table.
He held it in His right hand.
It contained the names of all who were a part of the Bride.
And when we saw him, we fell prostrate before Him.
He set the Book down, raised His hands and prayed.
His voice was strong, melodious, assuring and pleasant.
He prayed the wedding prayer –
"Blessed art Thou, O Lord our God, King of the Universe.
Thou hast created mirth and joy,
The Bridegroom and Bride,
Gladness and jubilation,
Dancing and delight,
Love, peace and fellowship.
O Lord our God, may the sound of mirth and joy be heard in the streets of Judah and Jerusalem.
Let the jubilant voice of Bridegroom and Bride be heard at this Feast.
Blessed art Thou, O Lord, who makes the Bridegroom rejoice with the Bride."

After this prayer He sat down at His table.
The greatest wedding feast of all time had begun.

THE WEDDING FEAST

It was an amazing experience to look across the vast expanse at this magnificent Bridal Chamber.
The walls were a pinkish pearl color about a thousand feet high.
Golden velvet drapes hung down from the ceiling to the floor.
They were perfectly spaced every several hundred feet. There were thousands of them.
On either side of the drapes were twelve feet wide and a hundred feet high pillars, reaching to the ceiling. They were covered with colorful precious stones set in fine gold carvings.
The floor was made of polished marble.
At the top of the walls where the ceiling met, were wide, artistically carved trim.
The highest point of the ceiling was in the middle of the Bridal chamber and it was thousands of feet high.
It tapered downward in cascades towards the sides.
Huge massive uniquely created diamond chandeliers hung from the ceiling.
They reflected the magnificent Godly light that filled the Chamber.
Millions of tables were arranged around the Chamber.
The legs of the wooden tables were artistically carved and made of a dark exotic wood.
There was a huge open space in the middle that could accommodate millions.

This was a Wedding Feast par excellence, never ever seen before.
The Heavenly cuisine for this Wedding Feast was unprecedented and supernaturally provided.

The tables were covered with the finest of linen and set with pure gold plates and cutlery.
The tables were decorated with fragrant flower arrangements.
These arrangements were made up of an assortment of -
White roses, Daffodils, Lily of the Valley, Honeysuckle, Apple Blossoms, White Heather, Jasmine, Orange Blossoms, Lavender and a variety of other beautiful flowers.
Wine glasses were set at every placing and there was an unlimited supply of new wine.
The glasses constantly remained full and the spread of food never ran out.
The most refined palates were delighted as they tasted the variety.
There were fruits, vegetables, cheeses, pastries, and other delicacies.
The guests enjoyed these tasty, delectable dishes that graced their plates.

Another amazing feature was the aspect of time.
Outside the New Jerusalem, time in terms of days and hours was Earthly.
Inside the New Jerusalem, time was eternal.
To everyone at the Wedding Feast time was irrelevant.
The program and activities proceeded in a very relaxed and comfortable way.

Tens of thousands of Angelic Musicians appeared above and their Orchestra graced the atmosphere with Heavenly Music.
They were dressed in white and gold.
They blended in with the beautiful décor.

Their musical instruments were of shining gold, silver and brass.
The mellifluous sounds of harpists, violins and stringed instruments harmonized in perfection.
It was glorious, soothing and satisfying.
A thousand genial composers could not together have created such a musical masterpiece.

Then Angel Choirs began to blend in with singing.
At times the chorus was Ancient Jewish, then Davidic Psalms and then Deep Spiritual Worship.
The music featured polyphonic compositions and the singing varied ranges of voices.
It was Divine.
I felt that the orchestra could keep playing and the choir keep singing forever.

Gabriel the Archangel stood to make an announcement.
He was huge and glorious.
His voice was strong and commanding.
As I looked at Him I realized, that He was the Messenger of God
He was the Archangel who throughout time had made important announcements to Humanity.
He spoke these words -
"The time has come for the Bride to speak to the Bridegroom.
It will be followed by the words of King David on behalf of all Israel."

The Bride speaks
The most precious words extolling Jesus were those of the Bride.

Millions of Saints were fascinated with their Heavenly Bridegroom.
Together as one voice we sounded these words of laudation and acclamation to Jesus -

You were slain, and have redeemed us to God by your blood.
You have chosen us out of every kindred, tongue, people and nation.
God has given us to be your Bride.
We belong eternally to You and are very thankful to God our Father.

You are the pure and holy Lamb of God
You love righteousness, and hate wickedness
As a man you were tempted yet without sin.
You overcame satan and triumphed over him openly.
You have the Keys of death and of hell.
Therefore our God has anointed you with the oil of gladness above everyone.

You are brave
You are the Great Messiah!
You entered the Eastern Gate of Jerusalem at your Second Coming.
All of Heaven and earth cried out -
"Lift up your heads, O ye gates and be ye lift up, ye everlasting doors.
And the King of glory shall come in.
Who is this King of glory?
The LORD strong and mighty
The LORD mighty in battle
The LORD of hosts, he is the King of glory."

THE WEDDING FEAST

You are beautiful
My beloved you are pure white and ruddy
You are the most beautiful of all of creation
You are fairer than the children of men and God hath blessed You forever
Your head is as the most fine gold
Your hair is white as wool
Your eyes are as the eyes of doves by the rivers of waters, washed with milk and fitly set
Your cheeks are as a bed of spices, as sweet flowers
Your lips like lilies dropping sweet smelling myrrh
Your hands are as gold rings set with beryl
Your belly is as bright ivory overlaid with sapphires.
Your legs are as pillars of marble, set upon sockets of fine gold
You stand in excellence as the cedars of Lebanon
Your mouth is most sweet and grace pours from your lips
All your garments smell of perfume, myrrh, aloes, cassia and everyone is made glad

You are wise
Your wisdom and knowledge by far exceeds that of Solomon
All that you have created demonstrates that
You do not keep all of your wisdom and knowledge to yourself
You share it and at your right hand you teach amazing things

You are powerful and glorious
Jesus of Nazareth, Son of the Living God
All power is given you in Heaven and on Earth
Who came from Edom and Bozrah? It was You.
All at Armageddon saw that You were glorious in apparel

THE APOCALYPSE THEN GLORY

You travelled in the greatness of your strength and You were mighty to save
Out of Your mouth a two-edged sword smote your enemies
You rode upon your white horse in majesty
You rode prosperously because of truth, meekness and righteousness
You cast the antichrist and false prophet into the lake of fire
You defeated satan, bound him and cast him into the bottomless pit

Truly, You were created in the form of God and thought it not robbery to be equal with God
Yet you made yourself of no reputation
You took on the form of a servant in the likeness of men
You humbled yourself and became obedient unto death, even the death of the Cross
Wherefore God has highly exalted You and given You a name which is above every name
At Your name Jesus, every knee bows that is in heaven, on the earth, and under the earth
Every tongue confesses that You are Lord, to the glory of God our Father.

You are Kingly
When you were suffering, Herod mocked and said – "Behold your King."
Now to his shame we say – "Behold our King."
You are greater and more glorious than all Kings who have ever reigned.
Your royal robe and magnificent train surrounds your Majestic Throne.

THE WEDDING FEAST

You are crowned with many Crowns of gold and glittering jewels.
We admire you as you sit in highest Authority, Honor, Dignity and Stateliness.
You reign as King of Kings.
Of your Kingdom there shall be no end.
You reign, execute judgment and justice in all the Earth.
Because of You all of Israel dwells safely.

Yes you are altogether lovely and You are my Beloved.
You are my Bridegroom and my Heavenly King.

At this time the Bride completed the words of admiration of Jesus.
They were spoken with complete love from our hearts.
Looking at Jesus, we could see that He was touched by what we said.
We were so glad to give Him joy.

Then each of the Saints lifted up their glass of wine to Jesus to toast Him and said –
"Shalom, Lichaim."
It means Peace and Life.

We all then sat down at our tables.
It became quite in the Banquet Chamber.

Sitting amongst the Special Guests was King David.
He stood up and proceeded to a special podium prepared for this occasion.

He spoke these words in praise of the Messiah saying -
Let all who live know that His name is The BRANCH;
He has built the Temple of the Lord: Even the temple that bears His glory.
He rules upon his Throne; and He is forever High Priest after the Order of Mechisidek.
It is He who has ascended on high, who led captivity captive and gave gifts unto men.
His scepter shall not depart from Judah, nor a lawgiver from between His feet.
He is Shiloh and unto him is the gathering of the people.
Unto us He is given: the Government is upon his shoulder,
His name is Wonderful, Counselor, The Mighty God, The Everlasting Father, The Prince of Peace.
He feeds his flock like a Shepherd and gathers the lambs with his arm.
He carries them in his bosom, and gently leads those that are with young.

Jesus Christ, You are the true Messiah -
You are fairer than the children of men.
Grace is poured into your lips.
Therefore God has blessed You forever.
The Spirit of the LORD rests upon You.
The Spirit of wisdom and understanding.
The Spirit of counsel and might.
The Spirit of knowledge and of the fear of the LORD.
You are quick in understanding and in the fear of the LORD
You rule over men justly and in the fear of God.
You are as the light of the morning and that light has replaced the sun.

THE WEDDING FEAST

Unto Israel I say -
Rejoice greatly, O daughter of Zion.
Shout, O daughter of Jerusalem: behold, your King has come unto you.
He is just, having salvation.

Then King David completed his praise of Jesus and went back to where he was sitting, to take his place amongst the other special guests.
After the speakers had spoken all these wonderful words of laudation, Jesus arose from where He was sitting and began to walk in the midst of the Bride
He walked down the aisles, between the bridal tables where millions of Saints were sitting.
There was joy, laughter and talking as everyone enjoyed the festivities.
As Jesus continued walking to each table, His eyes would make contact with each of the Saints.
With that came a loving smile from Jesus.
Each Saint inherently received a personal message from the Lord.
I experienced it and it was supernaturally transmitted to my heart.
It was loving, personal and deeply touching.
What a privilege it was to be able to see the Lord so close in all his magnificent glory.
I felt the vibrancy of His presence and it was electrifying.
We continued watching as the other Saints were also being greatly blessed.
Words cannot describe this amazing experience and I felt that it could continue forever.

Then Jesus moved to the central part of the Bridal Chamber.
He gestured for the Bride to come toward Him.
It was time for the Bridal Dance.
A Prophecy of David was about to be fulfilled.
Psalm 45:7-8
"Your God has set you above your companions by anointing you with the oil of joy.
All your robes are fragrant with myrrh and aloes and cassia.
From palaces adorned with ivory, the music of the strings makes you glad."

Jewish Weddings would be incomplete without the wedding dance.
It always plays a vital part of the wedding.
It is a fitting way to pay homage to the age old Jewish customs and traditions.

Millions of Saints formed a large circle around Jesus.
They then formed small dancing groups.
The dance began with slow music and a Yemenite kind of dance involving three steps.
Quick, quick and slow steps with a small pause on the last one.
Then there was a hopping and posturing Movement.
The music gained momentum and it became energetic, traditional music.

Then the music was accompanied with ecstatic singing
It was very similar to the Hava Nagila, with these words -
Let us rejoice
Let us rejoice

THE WEDDING FEAST

Let us rejoice and be happy
Let us sing
Let us sing
Let us sing and be happy
Rejoice, Bride rejoice
Rejoice Bride, with a happy heart
Rejoice Bride, rejoice Bride
Rejoice Bride, with a happy heart."

The dancers performed foot movements which included kicks and grapevine like steps.
There was bopping up and weaving as well.
The circle moved in and out, closing and then moving away from the Bridegroom.

There was great joy on the face of Jesus who then began to participate.
He raised both His arms and hands to each side and twirled as He danced.
He danced and danced and danced.
Eventually the dance was completed with great excitement everywhere.

Then Jesus raised His hands toward Heaven and said -
"My Father, it is for this joy that you set before Me, that I endured the cross and shame."

The voice of God the Father replied.
It sounded like many waters with these words -
"You are My beloved Son in whom I am well pleased."

There was a hush and everyone returned to their Tables and sat down.

Special small Wedding Cakes were then provided at each setting.
Each cake was decorated with an exquisite kind of frosting and wording.
Each represented the special qualities of perfect marriage such as -
Love, Purity, Faithfulness, Joy, Happiness, Peace and Gentleness.
We enjoyed these cakes and knew that the Wedding Blessings would follow.

Then the Sheva Brachot or Seven Wedding Blessings were pronounced

Mary the Mother of Jesus was ushered to where Jesus was.
She was a beautiful, gentle, loving and humble person.
She looked at Him first and then at the Bride.
She said –
"Let me speak special Wedding Blessings on the Bridegroom and the Bride."

1. Blessed art thou, O Lord our God, King of the Universe, who has created everything for His glory.

2. Blessed art thou, O Lord our God, King of the Universe, Who has created mankind.

3. Blessed art thou, O Lord our God, King of the Universe who hast made mankind in Thy image and likeness.

4. Blessed are You, O Lord who makes Zion joyful through her children.

THE WEDDING FEAST

5. Blessed art thou O Lord, who makes the Bridegroom and the Bride rejoice.

6. Blessed art thou, O Lord, our God, King of the Universe,
Who created joy and gladness, groom and bride, mirth, glad song, pleasure, delight, love, brotherhood, peace and companionship.
Lord, our God, let there soon be heard in the cities of Judah and the streets of Jerusalem the sound of joy and the sound of gladness, the voice of the Groom and the voice of the Bride, the sound of their jubilance.

7. Blessed art thou, O Lord, our God, King of the Universe,
Who gladdens the groom with the bride.

Then Mary finished the proclamation of blessings and Angel Hosts appeared everywhere.

Angelic praise to Jesus began.
It seemed as if the ceiling disappeared and the host reached into the Heavens.
They sang and praised God saying –
"Glory to God in the highest, and on earth peace, good will toward men.
Worthy is the Lamb that was slain.
He has received power, riches, wisdom, strength, honor, glory and blessing.
Hallelujah, for the Lord our God, the Messiah reigns.
Let us rejoice and be glad and give the glory unto Him.
Hallelujah, for the Lord our God the Messiah reigns."

The greatest Marriage Feast of all time was coming to a close.
The recessional was about to begin
Michael the Archangel appeared.
He stood there in full military regalia and spoke -
"This wonderful exciting event that we waited for so long and enjoyed has come to a close.
There will be a Prayer of Benediction.
Then the Bridegroom will leave to his Royal Quarters.
The Bride will then go to her Quarters.
The Special Guests will return to Heaven.
Then the Twelve Tribes of Israel will leave.
They will be followed by the International Guests.

Moses arose from his seat and came to the podium.
He stretched out his hands and gave the Benediction or Bracha.
It is the Aaronic or Priestly Blessing and Benediction. Numbers 6:24-26
"May the Lord bless and watch over You.
May the Lord cause His countenance to shine on You and favor You.
May the Lord raise His countenance toward You and grant You peace.
Amen."

After the Benediction, the main doors on the Eastern side of the Bridal Chamber opened again.
The Seven trumpeters stood there again with their golden trumpets.
There was a hush all over as everyone waited.

The moment had arrived for the Bridegroom to leave the Bridal Chamber.

THE WEDDING FEAST

The regal fanfare was played again on the long herald trumpets.
Again it brought a thrill as they played a new herald - "The King goes forth and He shall Reign."
They stood aside and Jesus Christ the Son of God, passed by them.
Then the 144,000 Jewish virgins followed dancing and left the Chamber.

The Bride leaves.
Just as we had arrived, so we also left in a timely, perfect and gracious way.
The Angels directed us to leave through the seven upper entrances.
We proceeded up the stairways leading out of the Chamber.

Heaven opened and the Special Guests were supernaturally translated back to Heaven.
The Israelites then left, tribe by tribe in orderly fashion.
Then the International Guests were ushered out.

At that time, all the festivities had ended and the Bridal Feast was over.

Words cannot describe our most amazing life with Jesus in the New Jerusalem.
It was only beginning and I knew that there was no end to its glory.

Chapter Twelve

Life in the New Jerusalem

We live in luxury and comfort.
Jesus provides everything we need or want.
It is exciting to serve Jesus and do our best for Him.
Each of us has been given individual assignments and responsibilities.

Some of the Saints were appointed as Ambassadors.
They presented a Message of Good News that Jesus wanted the World to know.
It made known all the blessings of His Glorious Kingdom.
It praised His greatness as King of Kings.
It revealed His compassion for Humanity.
It proclaimed the Laws of God.
It revealed the natural, physical and spiritual benefits people would experience if they embraced and obeyed the Laws of God.

Some Saints were given Special Priestly Assignments within the New Jerusalem.
These were performed on the Ceremonial and other days.
They also did service in Spiritual and Worship Gatherings.

The Earthly Priesthood was provided in the Temple in Jerusalem.
Those Priests ministered to the twelve Tribes of Israel.
They also provided special ministries of healing and miracles for people in the World.

This is exactly what God had promised -
"And hath made us priests unto God and his Father." Revelation 1:6
"Ye shall be named the Priests of the LORD: men shall call you Ministers of God." Isaiah 61:6

When Priests were appointed -
- They were carefully taught how to do their work.
- Their activities were perfectly scheduled
- They were given specific seasons, days and times of duty.
- These Priestly times of service were followed by seasons of rest.

Then there were many other kinds of assignments.
Some were sent to pick the healing leaves off the Trees of Life each month of the year.
They collected them in Cedar baskets and brought them to the Temple for keeping and distribution.

The leaves were distributed and used for the healing of sick people around the world.
Revelation 22:1-4.

Those who loved singing, got to be Singers at special events.
Some sang in Choirs.
There were those who served at Communion Services.
There were many Prayer Leaders who led prayer gatherings.
Some of the Saints were trained to be teachers of crafts.
These included Designing, Garments, Pottery, Weaving, Embroidery, Art and others.
There was also Furniture making, Gardening, Decoration, Jewelry design, Winemaking and Banqueting.
Some were selected to be Caregivers giving special care to Children.
There were many other exciting vocations and activities.

In all of our Appointments and Assignments, we were trained to do our work efficiently.
Each of us were given Angels to teach us, prepare us and help us.
It was exciting to work with them and enjoy such a wonderful relationship.

On one occasion I looked at the Angel working with me.
He was a tall and bright figure and His face was like translucent glass with rosy cheeks.
He had large blue eyes.

He had a perfect hairstyle of golden brown hair.
It was parted in the middle and hung neatly to his shoulders.
He was clothed in a shimmering white garment down to his feet.
He had a golden girdle around his waist and golden sandals on his feet.
He spoke with a soft, gentle, assuring voice.

Occasionally I could see other Angels glance at me.
It reminded me of the scripture where they asked God –
"What is man that Thou art mindful of him."
Hebrews 2:6
Angels always smiled and joined me in giving glory to God when I quoted Jude 24.
"I give praise to God who kept me from falling and presented me faultless before the presence of
his glory with exceeding joy."

My heavenly body and mind can do amazing things.
On earth I experienced many limitations.
Now in Heaven I have unlimited faculties and abilities.

We all gather together regularly for times of Spiritual Edification.

We enjoy Communion with Jesus frequently.
We always thank Him for coming to the Earth to rescue and save us.
Oh how wonderful it is to drink the New Wine with Him and keep the Passover.

Heavenly Music and Singing is always a part of our Spiritual Gatherings.
We experience rejoicing, happiness, praising and dancing with joy.
We always bow before the Lord and Worship Him.
At times we lay upon our faces before Him.
His presence then covers us and we feel the warmth of His anointing.

Individual and Corporate Prayer is a part of everyday life.
We enjoy wonderful times of corporate Prayer and it is special in this respect -
- We do not have to seek the Lords presence because we are in His presence.
- We do not have to pray for His Kingdom to come because it has come.
- We do not need to ask for forgiveness of sin because we are living in perfection.
- We do not ask to be delivered from evil because satan is bound in Sheol.

In our Prayers -
- We acknowledge God in all His greatness and our submission to Him.
- We worship God the Father, His Son Jesus Christ and the Holy Spirit.
- We thank God continuously for His Kingdom that has come.
- We are thankful that His will is being done on Earth as in Heaven.
- We want our devotion and service to Him to please Him.
- We thank Him for all His provisions and blessings.

We enjoy regular times of Teaching.
When on earth, Paul wrote these words -
"Eye hath not seen, nor ear heard, neither have entered into the heart of man, the things which God hath prepared for them that love him."
1 Corinthians 2:9
"Now I know in part; but then shall I know even as also I am known." 1 Corinthians 13:12

These words are now being fulfilled and I realize how much I did not know.
With great excitement, I receive the information and teachings provided for me.
I am experiencing new avenues and unending journeys of knowledge.
An eternal library of information has opened up to me.
Taking these excursions within time, eternity and beyond is fascinating.

It is always a joy to hear people speaking and sharing their testimonies.
Famous Biblical characters like Peter and Paul often speak.
They provide insight and commentaries which are so enlightening.
Saints like John and Charles Wesley sing their notable Hymns.
Church Fathers like Polycarp and Justin Martyr share their brave stories.
Humble Saints like William Booth and Mother Theresa speak of how they served the destitute.
It is good to listen to all of them.

A Major Highway was constructed from Egypt, to Jerusalem and on to Babylon.

LIFE IN THE NEW JERUSALEM

It passes by little towns and cities along the way.
It goes by Amman Jordan and on to Teheran.
The ruined city of Babylon was completely wiped off the map.
This new world renowned Highway was described by Isaiah the Prophet -
"When that time comes, there will be a highway between Egypt and Assyria. The people of those two countries will travel to and from between them, and the two nations will worship together. When that time comes, Israel will rank with Egypt and Assyria, and these three nations will be a blessing to all the world." Isaiah 19:23-25
Passing by Jerusalem, it fringes on the Beautiful Garden of Eden.
However people travelling down this Road are not permitted entry to Eden.
It is guarded by Mighty Angels.
Travelers passing by are left only to imagine its internal beauty.
They know that the Saints of God are allowed to enter and enjoy its beauty.

With great expectation I looked forward to my first visit to the Garden of the Great King.
I was told that nothing can compare with this Paradise that was created for us.

Leading to it, a special Highway descends from the New Jerusalem.
Isaiah prophesied about it –
"And a highway shall be there, and a way, and it shall be called the Way of holiness; the unclean shall not pass over it. Isaiah 35:8

Chapter Thirteen

Entering Eden

It was a wonderful experience to walk down this Highway and enter the Garden of the Lord.
We went in a group and Children accompanied us. Upon entering this wonderland, its freshness and natural beauty overwhelmed me.

THE APOCALYPSE THEN GLORY

It exceeded all descriptions of beauty.
It had a peaceful and quiet atmosphere.
Branching off were winding paths that led from it.

Along the paths were colorful flowers and fluttering Butterflies everywhere.
Here and there were Ladybirds and Honey bees moving from flower to flower.
I have always loved flowers and the fields were like bouquets everywhere.
There were colorful Tulips of all colors, more beautiful than any horticulturist could ever grow.
I saw Daffodils that had chrome yellow petals with deep orange inner cups.
The large sumptuous Peonies had a sweet scent with velvety, soft pink petals.
There were Irises with brilliant sky blue blooms and giant ruffled falls.
The white Lilies stood out amongst the red Carnations.
I smelt distinctive fragrances of Hyacinth and Wild Rose that perfumed the air.

In the background tiny insects were making their unique cricket like sounds.
We followed these paths to restful valleys with lush green pastures.
Here and there were white wool sheep and cattle grazing.
As I passed over a little hill, I saw the most breathtaking sight.
It was a rolling field of pink lavender as far as the eye could see.
The fragrance was wonderful.

There were several of us there and we sat down for hours enjoying each other's company and this stunning sight.
Eventually it was time to go home and we returned to the New Jerusalem.
Our return was an instantaneous experience.
We had the ability to travel at the speed of thought.
At the blink of an eye, we were back entering the City.

Fellowship
I always looked forward to the times of fellowship with other Saints.
Sometimes we walked and talked throughout the City.
On other occasions we visited with each other in our homes enjoying a meal.
I often received a visit from family members or friends.
We would just sit leisurely and enjoy a casual conversation.
On one occasion we talked about the Feast of Trumpets that was coming up.
Representatives from all over the World were coming and there would be great celebrations in Jerusalem.
While we were talking, my Mother pointed to a piece of clay pottery in one on the corners of the room.
It was about three feet high and I had these words inscribed on it -
"He is the Potter and I am the clay."
I kept it as an eternal reminder of the Lords work in my life.

Jesus always became the focal point of our conversation.
On earth I would say -
"If only I could have been one of the twelve Apostles with Christ in His earthly Ministry."
Now we were with Him in His amazing Kingdom.
We saw Him, we spoke to Him, we loved Him and we worshipped at His feet.
Everyone had something to say about Jesus.
We talked about His Kingly composure and the way He dressed.
Everyone was amazed at His infinite knowledge, what He said and the great wisdom He applied to every situation.
Our conversation would go on for hours.
We would bring food and drinks to the table and everyone enjoyed the meal.

Back to the Garden
I was glad when someone would say -
"Let's go visit Eden."
We entered and followed a path that led through beautiful valleys and meadows.
As we passed over a hill we came to luscious fields of green grass.
There before our eyes were thousands of animals grazing.
I saw magnificent black and white stallions among the horses.
One lifted his nose and nostrils to smell the fresh breeze.
As he did that he neighed and others followed with high and low pitched neighing.
There were baby foal and colts running and playing over the meadows.

I could see meandering streams winding through the fields.
A more beautiful sight one could not wish to behold.
Along the banks many of the animals were sitting and some were drinking.
We came to one of the streams and I sat down in the soft grass and looked into the water.

In this stream were different kinds of fish swimming.
They were clearly visible in the crystal clean water.
They moved with slow and sometimes darting movements.
There were Yellow Perch and Crappie.
I also saw some small and large Goldfish.
Rainbow Trout were making what seemed to be their upstream spawning run.
On the rocks on the side were little Snails moving slowly.
We sat down and enjoyed this peaceful sight for a long time.
Then we returned to the wonderful City of Light.

Once home again I enjoyed the comfort and pleasure of my Home.
One day I was reminiscing and reliving the joys that I had experienced.
An Angel who was a Messenger from the Lord entered to bring me a message.
In his hands he had a pure white garment with a girdle and sandals.
He instructed me to put them on and immediately accompany him to the Throne of Jesus.

THE APOCALYPSE THEN GLORY

He told me that because I was one of the many Overcomers we would receive special rewards and privileges.
I joined many others as we were led through the Palace.
Eventually we came to a large round entrance and waited.

The River of Life flows through it from the Throne.
On either side of the River are the Trees of Life.
On the outer side of them are two golden roads that lead to the Throne.
The distance from the entrance to the Throne is about one mile.
On either side of the roads are galleries that reach high up.
Close to the Throne on either side, thousands of Angels are seated.

The Throne of Jesus is made of pure white marble.
Seven steps lead to a platform in front of it.
Behind the Throne are galleries that are thousands of feet high.
They are filled with hundreds of thousands of Angels.
Their orchestras play and choirs sing Praise to Jesus Christ.
A soft Golden Misty Light fills the vast area.

We were told that it was time to enter the Throne Room.
We walked down one of the golden roads on the side of the River of life.
It took a while to reach the Throne.

ENTERING EDEN

We approached Jesus on His Throne and it was an illustrious experience.
At first the brightness of His Presence was overwhelming.
It took me several minutes to adjust to it.
Jesus had arranged special places around His Throne for us.
We sat there overwhelmed by His Glorious presence.
It was amazing to look around and see its magnificence.
It is the most majestic Throne Room ever created.

Jesus spoke to us as a group.
He told us about several rewards He was giving us -.
- First we would be allowed to go into paradise and enjoy the fruit of the Tree of Life.
- We would also be allowed to enter the Temple at different times.
- At times we were permitted entrance to the Manna Room to taste and eat of the Hidden Manna.

Then Jesus spoke to each of us individually.
This made my relationship with Jesus so indescribably personal and special.
He gave me a white stone with my new secret name written in it.
He told me that at the times of His choosing, I would be allowed to walk with Him.
Then at this time I would wear a shimmering white Overcoming Garment that He gave me.

Then He spoke a word and something unique happened to me.

Supernaturally, the following names were written on me -
- The Name of God,
- The New Name of Jesus
- The name New Jerusalem

I fell at His feet and humbly thanked Him.
It was such a deeply moving and special moment for me.

Eventually, when Jesus had finished, we were ushered out of His presence.
I returned to my Mansion.

I wanted to go back to the Garden.
The occasion arose and we returned to Eden.
This time we visited a place where the Springs of Water are.
This is where the bubbling and gurgling waters flow out of the ground.
They form little streams that flow down the hillsides to a large lake.
The lake is calm with placid waters.
They reflect the blue sky, cloud formations and distant mountains.
Near the shore there were ducks and swans swimming together.
I saw Great Blue Heron and Storks wading in the shallow water.
On the bank a mama duck was giving her little ones a swimming lesson.
As she waddled they followed her with a splash, back into the water again.

In the distance I could see huge snow covered mountain peaks.
There grandeur far surpassed that of the Swiss or Bulgarian Alps.
They towered above the snow covered mountain slopes.
Below were mountains and valleys carpeted in green vegetation.
On the left I could see colorful cathedral like rock formations.

I lay on my back in the soft green grass and looked up.
I could see Eagles gliding majestically high up in the sky.
At a lower level were Canadian Geese flying in their typical v formation.
I looked backwards at the New Jerusalem and it was so large.
Its sides reached high, beyond the blue sky into the Heavens.
Again it was time to go Home and we were all happy to do so.

The New Jerusalem was a happy place.
On one occasion many of us gathered together in one of the Fellowship Rooms.
We talked about our joys of living.
It was so wonderful to know that there were no goodbyes or farewells.
We were with each other forever.
Moms, Dads, Children, Bothers, Sisters, Husbands, Wives, Grandparents, Relatives and Friends could see each other anytime.

THE APOCALYPSE THEN GLORY

We also enjoyed talking and sharing our thoughts and experiences with each other.
How thankful I was that there were no time limitations.

On one occasion we went as a group to the River of Life.
It proceeded from the Lords Throne.
We went to pick and eat fruit on the Tree of Life.
At the speed of thought we found ourselves standing next to the River of Life.
What an amazing reward this was that the Jesus had given to us.
It was a fulfillment of one of the promises -
"Blessed are they that do his commandments that they may have right to the tree of life." Revelation 22:14

I stood at the bank and looked down at the water of this crystal clear River.
I looked toward my right and saw that it proceeding out of a bright light.
This was the throne of God and of the Lamb.
We walked and talked as we went.
In the midst and on either side of the river, we were able to pick and enjoy eating fruit.
We are allowed to do this each month enjoying the twelve different kinds of fruit each year.
We were doing what Adam and Eve had done in the Garden of Eden.
An interesting fact about this River of Life is the following -
- It flows in an easterly direction into the sea.
- Wherever it comes it brings life and healing to the waters and every living, moving creature.

Ezekiel 47:1-12.
That day was a wonderful day well spent and then we returned to the New Jerusalem.

The New Jerusalem is an interesting place.
One of the things that I should mention is the huge Library that is available to all.
It is a place frequently visited.
It provides perfect and complete information on any subject.
Innumerable Books are available to read.
We often took time to share with each other the amazing things we had read and learnt.

We would also reminisce about life in Heaven after the rapture.
About the many wonderful things we had seen, heard and experienced there.
We talked about the New Jerusalem.
It is huge and each floor has about 2 million square miles of space.
It would take a long time to discover all it has to offer.
It has spectacular designs, accommodations and amenities.

The New Jerusalem is an eternal experience and time is not of the essence.
Outside of our own work assignments and leisurely activities there are many places to visit. There we can see others working and showing their expertise.
We can watch the children at play with their caregivers.
We may listen to the Choirs preparing for their recitals.

I always love going to one of the Refreshing pools to enjoy the cool crystal clear water.
There are many of them and each one is uniquely different.
There are variations of bubbling, flowing, spraying or wavelike water.
Some are surrounded by various nature settings and others designed like Artesian Baths.
They provide relaxation and enjoyment, far surpassing anything I had ever enjoyed on Earth.

I also greatly enjoy watching talented Saints making Pottery, designing Garments, Weaving or doing intricate Embroidery.
Furniture making has always fascinated me and I like watching Craftsman making furniture.
It is interesting to see them carefully assemble the pieces.
An amazing place worth visiting is where the artists come together and do all kinds of painting.
The Artists in the New Jerusalem are the best I have ever known.
Their painting procedures, techniques and finished works of art are breathtaking.

All of these talented workers bring great blessing in the New Jerusalem.
Without doubt I can say, there is never a dull or boring moment here.

Back to the Garden
On another occasion we returned to visit the Forests.
We came to a waterhole about a mile in diameter.
It was surrounded by grassland and bush.

ENTERING EDEN

Forests fringe on the grasslands.
Out of the forests hundreds of animals were coming down to the waterhole.
I could see a Black Bear and a Gray Wolf and they were grazing together.
The grass looked like a combination of Kentucky bluegrass and Bermuda grass.
There were Zebras everywhere.
I saw a Cheetah and two Tigers and alongside them a herd of Elephants.
Many of the animals were drinking at the waterhole.
I walked to where the Tigers were laying in the grass.
One was nursing her baby Cubs.
They were tame and docile.
I sat next to them and softly stroked their fur and they were friendly.
They purred with a deep sounding purr.
I was fascinated as I looked closely at the fur.

It varied in color from yellow to dark burnt orange.
It was covered with an abundance of wider and narrower black stripes.

Then we walked between the animals.
I discovered an amazing thought communication between us and them.
They welcomed us and were thankful we were there.
Creation had waited a long time for the manifestation of the Sons of God.

On the other side of the lake were Hippopotami swimming and chasing each other.

Lions and White Tailed Deer were drinking water together at the water's edge.
There were magnificent Peacocks strutting around with their colorful fantailed feathers.
Near to that was the edge of the forest.
I saw Monkeys swinging on vines from tree to tree.
There were squirrels darting up and down the tree boughs.
Beneath, rabbits were hopping through the tall grass.
The trees were full of fruits and flowers and were most inviting.
We walked into the forest.
There were different kinds of wild berries to be picked and enjoyed everywhere.
As I walked I became aware of something amazing.
I could hear the trees whispering praises to the Creator and extolling God.
Birds were flying from tree to tree, perching on branches, chirping and singing.
There were a great variety of them that I recognized.
Goldfinch
Bluebirds
Cardinals
Woodpeckers
Song Sparrows
Swallows and Doves.
I stretched out my hand and a bluebird came and sat in my hand.
A dove came and perched on my shoulder.
There was a wonderful connection between the trees, plants, critters, birds and animals.
They were peacefully communicating with each other and giving praise to God.

ENTERING EDEN

They rejoiced that the Kingdom of Jesus had come and the Children of God were in their midst.

As we continued to walk we saw many different kinds of trees in the forest.
They had different shapes, sizes and colors.
There were
Oak,
Magnolia,
Cedar,
Dogwood,
Hickory,
Redbud,
Pine,
Spruce,
Chestnut,
Sweet gum and
Walnut.
All kinds of fruit trees were scattered everywhere and they were covered with delicious fruit.
There were Apple trees with red apples and golden pears on Pear trees.
I saw yellow oranges hanging on Orange trees and ripe blush red peaches all over Peach trees.
Close by I noticed a Mulberry tree.
I helped myself and picked delicious fruit to my heart's content.

Close by was a stream and on the bank there were Willow trees.
Their branches were swaying in the breeze and I went and sat under one of them.
I watched the swirling water, winding around the rocks, flowing downstream.

THE APOCALYPSE THEN GLORY

The Four Rivers of the Paradise Garden.
From Jerusalem through Paradise are Four Rivers that flow to the four corners of the Earth.
Their original names have been kept as they were in the original Garden of Eden.

First is the Pison.
It flows westward toward the United States.
This river has gold, bdellium and onyx stone everywhere.
The swirling water flows between rocks, cascading down waterfalls, into pools along the way.
It is exciting to look for and pick up glimmering gold nuggets from the bottom of the pools.
The pools are always teaming with fish.
Looking in the shallow water between the rocks, one may find sparkling diamonds, rubies, emeralds, blue sapphires and other precious stones.
We all love collecting them in a treasure trove, letting the children play with them.
Then they drop the stones one by one into the water and watch them sink to the bottom.

Second is the Gihon.
It passes southward to Ethiopia and then on to Africa.

Third is the Hiddekel.
It flows northward towards Europe.

Fourth is the Euphrates.
Its course is eastward through Iran toward China.

Meandering out of these huge Rivers are smaller tributaries.

They flow to all the Countries of the Earth.
The World therefore has an abundant water supply.
Everywhere the vegetation is green, lush, blossoming and fruitful.

Visiting the Garden that Jesus gave us is always an unforgettable experience.
Going back to the New Jerusalem and my gorgeous Mansion is equally great.

We often speak of how fortunate we are to experience this Wonderful Life.

How sad it is that many may miss this opportunity!

I pray that the pages of this book may bring a new beginning and future for you!

In conclusion:
This book describes future events that have been prophesied and will soon come to pass.
Because they are yet to be fulfilled, you still have the opportunity to choose a great destiny.
You can ensure that your future is a Glorious One.
You may also be a part of the Bride of Christ.
You may receive many wonderful awards.
You may also live in the New Jerusalem forever.

I invite you to respond to this Wedding Invitation today -

The Most High God of the Heavens and the Earth

invites you

to be a part of the Bride of His Son Jesus Christ

to live in His eternal Glory

in the New Jerusalem with Jesus Christ, the King of Kings

Experience this by following these easy instructions:

How to become a Christian

1. **Know that God loves you.**
Gods love is a real kind of love that does something wonderful for us.
When God saw mans hopeless, desperate sinful condition, he decided to help man.
He lovingly gave His only Son to die and be crucified for us on the Cross.
Even though Jesus was innocent, He paid the price for our salvation.
John 3:16
"For God so loved the world that He gave His only begotten, Son that whosoever believeth on Him should not perish, but have everlasting life."
2. **Know that all have sinned.**
Everyone has committed at least one sin in their life and that makes us all sinners.
We all stand guilty before God.
Rom 3:23
"For all have sinned and come short of the glory of God."
3. **Know that Jesus Christ is the only way.**
There are people that teach that there are different ways to God and Heaven.
This is not true. Jesus said that He is the only way.
John 14:6
"I am the way the truth and the life; no man cometh unto the Father, but by me."
Jesus is the only way for you to receive forgiveness and salvation..
4. **Know that today is your day of salvation.**
The only moment that we are sure of is *now*.

Yesterday is gone, and tomorrow may not come.
If we accept Jesus Christ now we will be saved.
2 Corinthians 6:2
"Now is the accepted time, now is the day of salvation."
Proverbs 27:1
"Boast not thyself of tomorrow; for thou knowest not what a day may bring forth."
5. **Receive Jesus Christ as your Savior now.**
Invite Jesus to come into your life now and you will experience the following:
- All your sins will be forgiven.
- Jesus will cleanse you from all sin with His precious Blood.
- God the Father will accept you as His own Child.
- God will write your name in His Book of Life.
- God will give you everlasting life.
- You will experience a personal relationship with Jesus and He will never leave you.

Please make this decision now and pray this prayer:

Dear Jesus, I invite you to come into my life right now.
Please forgive all my sins and cleanse me with your precious Blood.
I accept you as my Lord and Savior.
Please reveal Yourself to me, and become real in my life from this moment.
Please write my name in Your Book of Life and give me everlasting Life.
I ask this in Your wonderful Name - Jesus
Amen.
If you prayed this prayer:
Find a Bible-believing Church to attend regularly.
Read your Bible and pray every day.

Other Books that have been published by Ken Wooldridge:

24 Doctrines of the Bible
It is convenient to have all of these Doctrines under one cover
It also helps to make them easy to understand
It helps those who want to know what the Bible teaches, so that they can experience and proclaim Bible truth.

Understanding the End Times
By reading this book, one is confronted with the following questions:
What is the true timeline of the World.
What major world events are about to happen?
How will our lives be affected?
How can we prepare ourselves?
How can we ensure our salvation and escape?

Living in difficult times
Ken Wooldridge was born in Botswana and raised in Africa
He has been living in Tennessee for over twenty years
He has learned the benefits of foraging wild edible and medicinal plants
This book includes hard to find recipes
It contains a vast amount of other valuable information

These books will help you and those you love

Available at www.amazon.com
Available at www.amazon.com/Kindle-eBooks

www.ingramcontent.com/pod-product-compliance
Lightning Source LLC
Chambersburg PA
CBHW061644040426
42446CB00010B/1572